Arms Out, Palms Open

Conflict, Reconciliation, and Gay Inclusion

DAPHNE G. ESTWICK

Morehouse Publishing

NEW YORK · HARRISBURG · DENVER

Unless otherwise marked, all Scriptures are from the King James Version of the Bible.

Quote on page iv by William Sloane Coffin from *The Collected Sermons of William Sloane Coffin – The Riverside Years, Volume 2* (Louisville, KY: Westminister John Knox Press, 2008), 15.

Morehouse Publishing, 4775 Linglestown Road, Harrisburg, PA 17112

Morehouse Publishing, 445 Fifth Avenue, New York, NY 10016

Morehouse Publishing is an imprint of Church Publishing Incorporated.

www.churchpublishing.org

Cover design by Laurie Klein Westhafer
Typeset by Denise Hoff

Library of Congress Cataloging-in-Publication Data

Estwick, Daphne G.
    Arms out, palms open: conflict, reconciliation, and gay inclusion / Daphne G. Estwick.
        p. cm.
    Based on the dissertation (Ed. D. -- Columbia University)
    Includes bibliographical references and index.
    ISBN 978-0-8192-2758-4 (pbk.) -- ISBN 978-0-8192-2759-1 (ebook)
    1. Church work with gays. 2. Homosexuality -- Religious aspects -- Christianity. 3. Gays -- Religious life. 4. Clergy--Sexual behavior. I. Title.
    BV4437.5.E88 2012
    259.086'64 -- dc23

                    2011043813

Printed in the United States of America

10 9 8 7 6 5 4 3 2 1

For God hath not given us the spirit of fear;
but of power, and of love, and of a sound mind.

—2 Timothy 1:7

"Self-surrender is the proper attitude to life in general, simply because life finally can't be earned or grasped with fists clenched, it can only be received with palms open."

—William Sloane Coffin

❈ DEDICATION ❈

This book is dedicated to Father Richard Gressle and all the priests, deacons, ministers, pastors, rabbis, imams, monks, nuns, and clergy of all faiths who daily and dutifully, quietly or passionately, through their presence or their prayers, extend themselves with arms out, palms open to help others enter a better place.

Contents

Part I | Who They Were

Part 2 | What They Learned

Part 3 | The Challenges They Faced

Part 4 | How They Learned

Part 5 | What It All Means for Clergy and for Us

Acknowledgments

A great many people, moments, situations, and circumstances contribute to any research and writing effort. These individuals included below are just a few who have helped me in this process. I am thankful to:

Catherine and Randolph Estwick, for their elevated expectations.

Louise Robbins for her encouragement and willingness to focus on the details.

Marie Volpe, the perfect adviser at just the right time.

Javier Viera, for uttering the words I was afraid to speak and telling me I could turn my dissertation into a book.

Donia Allen, for offering unbridled encouragement.

Davis Parker, for believing in an unknown author.

Jane and Rick Wolff for their collaborative efforts on my behalf.

Peggy L. Curchack, for her unwavering enthusiasm and support.

Daryl Hairston and Jennifer Austin, as the memory of their generosity continues to bring out the best in me.

I am especially thankful to the clergy who participated in this research project as they met me with open arms and open hearts.

Preface

Conflict knows no boundaries. It crosses religious, racial, geographic, socioeconomic, and other forms of separation imposed on our society. Individuals from assorted walks of life are confronted with conflicts they must resolve. Yet many enter negotiations propelled by fear. We feel powerless and often anticipate an unsatisfactory outcome. Such fears can be shared by disputants and negotiators alike and by men and women with a range of professional experiences. How, I wondered, might individuals who bring a religious perspective, such as clergy, go about reaching resolutions and reconciliations in their own personal and professional lives? What approach might they take and what resources might they tap into to become effective negotiators?

There is an unspoken expectation that much can be learned from religious leaders. When facing a national or personal crisis, we often turn to rabbis, imams, priests, ministers, and other spiritual leaders for guidance. Yet why do so many of us approach them only in a time of crisis? If they help us translate complex theological understandings into practical daily applications, might not their perspectives also help the rest of us as well as other clergy move through an array of difficult circumstances?

What special skills might they bring to conflict resolutions? Given the nature of their profession, I thought there could very well be something to learn if only we could place their experiences under a microscope. Could they provide us with any insights into how disagreeing parties can successfully navigate potentially explosive terrain—while keeping our innermost values intact? The question of whether or not to fully embrace gays within the Church has been an especially explosive issue, one that has generated a great deal of conflict. In addition, while there are studies that focus on the general responsibilities of clergy, there is little research available on the impact clergy have had on parishioners concerning their interactions with gays. Nor is much written concerning how clergy learn to manage such responsibility. So my chosen topic seemed worth exploring on any number of fronts.

I began by searching for clergy who had successfully negotiated especially difficult disputes, hoping their experiences would offer new perspectives on the most effective skills needed to reach resolutions. Very little is known about the nature of those skills that are most effective in constructive conflict resolutions.

In dealing with emotionally driven conflicts, like those generated in response to the push for increased gay rights within the Church and society-at-large, we often struggle as we attempt to answer three overarching questions. Based on the experiences of clergy in both their personal and professional lives, this book reveals clerical responses to these questions and is also designed to help others answer:

1. What is an **ideal response to conflict**? Which characteristics and attitudes reflect that response and what skills should I cultivate, particularly if I am a person of faith?

2. What are the **greatest challenges** I am likely to face as I attempt to resolve conflicts?

3. What **practical steps can I take** to learn how to address these challenges?

A retrospective glimpse of my own responses to conflict leaves me somewhat embarrassed and amused. All parties involved would have been much better served had I paused to ask *any* of the questions listed above. Though not a priest, I have come to realize that there is an ideal set of conflict responses that reflect my espoused values. Unfortunately, at times there has been a disconnect between my actions and supposed beliefs. In spite of the difficulties involved, I continue to strive to integrate the two. The experiences shared by clergy interviewed for this book reflect not only their successes, but their struggles as well. Insights stemming from the challenges they faced, along with tangible guidelines for ways to address these challenges are shared.

My primary aim is to provide readers with a useful framework for resolving conflicts—a framework that is grounded in fundamental Christian principles. In part to address my own deficiencies, I wanted to get a better sense of how one's values can positively inform efforts to resolve conflicts. The individual conflict resolution and reconciliation experiences of clergy shared here provide a perspective that has not previously been examined nor critically assessed.

This distillation of clerical experiences is offered for those attempting to remain true to the values conveyed in the open posture of a priest regardless of whether or not one operates in a religious or a secular sphere. The primary emphasis is on understanding the strategies employed by clergy in order to help others as they struggle to resolve difficult conflicts. It should also be noted that this book is not designed to replace comprehensive works from experts in the field of conflict studies. Rather, it is a supplemental guide based on the conflict resolution strategies of clergy. It is designed to assist those who wish to resolve conflicts by utilizing a spiritually oriented approach. A list of secular readings, however, is included in the bibliography.

In listening to the experiences of clergy, a number of themes began to emerge. Those themes provide the foundation of this book, which is divided into corresponding sections. The discoveries made by the clergy I spoke with and the strategies they employed involved a sometimes seemingly contradictory set of steps. Yet I found there was much to be learned from their approach. Their perspective is especially applicable in situations where the long-term relationships are greater than, and for a variety of reasons must supersede, the immediate disagreement.

The most successful patterns to emerge were the ones that evolved over time. Efforts to resolve the conflict generally followed an approach that included:

1. **Assuming the posture of a priest:** They let go of preconceived notions and became centered as they adopted an "arms out, palms open" posture that conveyed a willingness to listen.

2. **Focusing on a higher plane:** Somewhat counterintuitively, they looked above the fray and fixed their glance firmly, rather than be distracted by the many challenges and obstacles that had the capacity to take them off course.

3. **Learning to tread carefully:** They learned to move through a host of social interactions with patience and deliberately placed steps.

The three phases of their approach correspond to sections two, three, and four of this book. Section five includes a summary and recommendations. It is worth noting that the starting point of arms out, palms open was what clergy often returned to throughout conflict negotiations. It was also the most crucial in terms of their success. This arms out, palms open posture of a priest served as the ideal place of departure and return. It helped to establish and reinforce the most appropriate tone for negotiations. As Osmond, with his thirty-five years of ministry, said:

> I would point out that the posture for a priest is at the altar, arms out, palms open. A boxer has fists clenched. If you go from arms out, palms open, it's vulnerable. They'll put steel through those palms. But if you don't close with fists clenched, if you sustain that [open posture], you increase the chances in my judgment of not only hearing them better, but them realizing they're being heard.

In the midst of emotionally laden conflicts, it is understandably quite difficult to adopt such an accepting and loving stance. Yet it is precisely with this arms out and palms open approach that clergy demonstrated the skills that were needed most—allowing love to conquer fear. The skills utilized in this process of reconciliation and resolution also resemble the best approach taken when crossing a tightrope. Successful movement across a high wire requires an open and balanced posture, a focus on what matters most and learning to take slow and deliberate steps.

Part I | Who They Were

The population included an agile and diverse group of individuals. Their ability to respond to a variety of circumstances was important as the process of resolving conflicts more often resembles a carnival act than it does a singular and love-filled gesture. Frequently we may feel as if we are suspended in midair while being encouraged to cross a thin wire extended high above the ground. Who wouldn't be frightened? Yet conflict links our present moment of distress to the peaceful place at the other end of the wire we hope to reach, once the conflict is resolved. In an ideal scenario our wide smile gleams in the spotlight. We reach our destination gracefully, with class and perhaps even a bit of flare as the audience goes wild with applause. In reality, however, we often hope for dimmed lights, few observers, and want nothing more than to be transported from one side to the other, without being required to take that first step of uncertainty.

Many of the men and women I spoke with were, at some point, quite reluctant to step out and negotiate a conflict. There was an underlying recognition that fear and a lack of preparation can lead to inertia or, even worse, to a hastily and poorly executed strategy with seemingly fatal results. Thus, there is hesitation. The wire seems so narrow, the ground so far away, and our feet feel so unsteady. Yet by assuming the posture of a priest, it is possible to feel empowered and sufficiently balanced to move beyond our fears and take the first step

In analyzing the various approaches taken by clergy, I discovered that there were very specific attitudes they conveyed and very concrete skills they developed. I was surprised by the range of experiences they brought not just to the individual conflicts we discussed, but also to their respective ministries. While they came from many different backgrounds, only a few had received special training designed to help them resolve conflicts. The majority had not received such preparation. Yet what they generally had in common was an overarching understanding of the power of love. This was demonstrated most often by their attitude of inclusiveness. With this they brought a willingness to entertain ambiguities along with an informal approach to learning that allowed them to refine their skills and their approach one step, or misstep, at a time.

So what was the ideal priestly response that launched them lovingly though the conflict? Which characteristics most encapsulated that response? One should make no mistake, it was not all flowers and sunshine. Listening to their stories, common threads surfaced through a host of challenges. One key theme involved the challenge to balance multiple competing demands. As is the case in crossing a tightrope, the ideal posture was one that allowed them to find their center and remain balanced—in the case of clergy, balanced between vulnerability and strength. In the middle of these two seemingly contradictory realms, balance was achieved only as they stood with arms open wide. While they were vulnerable to attacks from many sides, they were at the same time strengthened by way of a Higher Power.

The characteristics of those who adopted this posture, thereby gaining strength, reflected very specific attitudes and skills, all of which were described as being part of an ongoing process of development. So, for example, the ability to listen actively was presented not as an end point, but rather as an ongoing learning process. It was spoken of as something our very human nature required us to continually refine.

We learn to crawl before we learn to walk and the ability to cross a tightrope comes only with practice. For most of us the primary desire, if compelled to walk across a high wire, would be simply to reach the other side quickly and intact. Taking slow and deliberate steps with arms open wide might feel like counterintuitive moves, but they are actually the most prudent. As demonstrated by the clergy interviewed for this book, strategies that incorporate these approaches require effort, but they certainly can be learned. The experiences shared in chapter 1 and throughout this book reflect individual struggles to remain true to the posture of a priest. Such efforts can serve as a model for us all.

CHAPTER I

Questioning Clergy

The following conflict profiles introduce clergy with unique personal histories. Concerning their ability to resolve conflicts, each began as a novice who initially fell short of his or her expectations. Only one, Dean, displayed an innate affinity for conflict negotiations at an early age. Encouragingly, there was no particular background or inherent personality that emerged as being superior to others with regard to resolving conflicts. Regardless of background, each person developed and improved with experience.

It is worth noting that the adoption of the arms out, palms open stance was not limited to ordained priests who shared a common history. Of the sixteen members of the clergy I interviewed, one was an ordained deacon and one was a Methodist minister with long-standing ties to the Episcopal Church. The remaining fourteen men and women were ordained Episcopal priests from distinctly different backgrounds, ranging in age from their forties to their eighties. As they discussed suitable approaches to a variety of conflicts, the importance of the arms out, palms open posture emerged as an underlying and universal theme that joined them together regardless of gender, age, or prior experiences.

I was surprised by the range of life experiences the men and women I interviewed brought to their ministry. Though equally divided by gender, they each came with a unique personal history. For some, serving as an Episcopal priest had been their sole and long-term career. Others spent a significant number of years in a variety of professions.

Several had spent time overseas. One worked as a missionary in sub-Saharan Africa. One was a former member of the radical 1960s group the Students for a Democratic Society, while another had lived in a convent as a nun, and another worked as a flight attendant for many years. Gym teacher, marketing specialist, registered nurse, and head of a nonprofit organization were also positions held at one time or another by the men and women I interviewed. Some attended Episcopal seminaries, others did not. Some entered the seminary directly from college, others did not. Some attended seminaries known for their liberal views. Others attended those seen as more conservative. Some had a calm disposition. Some were feisty and became quite animated as they discussed a conflict they were called to resolve.

As singular as their personalities and their experiences may have been, a number of common points surfaced in the strategies they designed and in the lessons they learned. Each struggled in their attempts to resolve a conflict issue. Some were more successful or more confident than others, but they each seemed to emerge from this struggle stronger and better able to apply relevant skills in subsequent conflict encounters. A few even appeared surprised to identify the extent of their growth in this area as I asked questions that prompted them to reflect. Only then did they seem to appreciate just how far they had come in their ability to bring about reconciliation and resolutions without the high level of anxiety that had accompanied their efforts in the past.

The road leading to such discoveries was not without its share of difficult steps and missteps accompanied by doubt. Not only did I question the clergy, it turned out that they also questioned themselves. With regard to the conflicts they had resolved, many looked with skepticism at some aspect of the status quo, whether it was in their personal or professional lives. They admitted that at one time or another they carried an ample load of self-doubt into their conflict negotiations. For some the process resembled the actions of a person groping for the exit in a darkened, smoke-filled room. Yet initial panic gave way to reliance on that which was greater than their fears or the conflict itself. In doing so, their options increased. With time, and through the process of learning, their movements became much more deliberate and refined.

It has been said that if one wants to walk on the water, then one must first step off the boat. In their efforts to resolve conflicts, many of the clergy I spoke with were willing to do just that as they placed themselves in a position of vulnerability. The willingness to take the first step off the boat, and the faith that this required, remained evident regardless of whether it was to welcome an AIDS program no other congregations wanted, or to extend a hand that was bitten by changes in church policies or quite literally by a fellow clergy member.

There was a general recognition that a connection beyond their religious identity would sustain them through difficult times. The posture of a priest encompassed more than the mere donning of appropriately elaborate robes. As reflected in their comments, the most suitable posture included a vulnerable stance, a diminished personal agenda, and ultimately a willingness to remain open to the Holy Spirit. It was a nonthreatening posture that conveyed openness and love. Clergy needed to first reconcile themselves with the posture of a priest before they could set out on a successful journey. This posture had a dual purpose. It centered them while it also conveyed their willingness to listen.

While their goal was to remain centered, clergy approached this target from many different angles. Not every seasoned priest found it easier than those less experienced to bring about reconciliations. In some instances those relatively new to ministry were able to contextualize the conflict and reach that centered posture by drawing upon what they experienced in prior nonministerial careers. Each brought something different to the table. With their strengths and weaknesses intertwined, they were able, at some point, to reach reconciliation or ultimately a resolution. Thus it was not so much what they brought, but how they utilized what they were given and the attitude they adopted that were of greatest importance.

The following conflict profiles included below serve as an introduction to the individuals interviewed for this book and reflect the diversity of experience these members of the clergy brought with them. The specific skills and attitudes they found most effective in addressing these and other conflicts are discussed in detail in chapters 2 and 3.

In each of the conflict profiles, clergy speak candidly of their struggles to become more attuned to the appropriate course of action. Their distinct personalities are apparent even in these very brief vignettes. Yet what is most helpful to remember is that while they took many different paths, they each learned to assume the posture of a priest and have improved in their efforts to successfully negotiate conflict. If they, this oddly assorted group of individuals, were able to do so, might not we be able to do so as well?

At the start of the interview, each person was asked to respond to a conflict scenario in which they were called to resolve a difficult issue within their parish. The scenario resembled a General Ordination Examination question, and it prompted them to synthesize a number of interrelated issues.

Conflict Scenario

Imagine yours is a small financially challenged but socially, ethnically, and economically diverse congregation. You are approached by two gay members of your church and asked to officiate at their commitment ceremony. They would like your permission to hold that ceremony in the church sanctuary. They have discussed their plans to approach you with other members of the congregation and sentiments are evenly divided. Half the members are supportive. The other half—coincidently, the same members who offer the greatest financial support for the church—have threatened to leave the congregation should such a ceremony take place. Based on your experiences, what steps might you now take to resolve this proposed conflict if faced with it today?

As each interviewee walked through the steps they would take, they often began to discuss related conflicts. Each was then asked to briefly describe a specific incident where he or she had personally been involved in resolving a conflict that related to homosexuality. In an effort to offer some privacy, pseudonyms have been assigned to the clergy interviewed for this book.

Grant

Thirty-eight years of ministry, Episcopal Divinity School

I was not surprised to learn that Grant had been a former member of Students for a Democratic Society (SDS), nor that he had been trained as a community organizer. Though now in his sixties, with the trim, fit physique of a cyclist and apparent enthusiasm for life, Grant still exuded the energy of a student activist. Although his pace was quick, he provided long, thoughtful responses to each question. Apparently comfortable enough in his own skin, he was not afraid to reveal his struggles as well as his successes.

Over the course of his ministry, Grant resolved many conflicts. One that related to gay inclusion, and seemed to engender the strongest emotions, involved the opening of a center in his parish for anyone with AIDS. While the disease affected a number of populations, in the early years it was often associated with gay men. During the height of the AIDS epidemic, Grant said his parish was approached by an Episcopal layman from New York who was searching for an appropriate venue where a variety of social service programs might be offered. Three other churches in the county had turned down this gentleman. Funding was available to provide a full array of social services and to support the program. Yet acceptance of such a program within the parish went far beyond finances. Offering such services might have appeared to be a natural extension of the church, but there were protocols to be followed.

Grant first brought the proposal to the wardens, then to the vestry, then to key congregants, and ultimately to the entire congregation. Responses varied from supportive to hostile. As he recounted these experiences, it was clear that the conflict resolution process had been both personally and congregationally painful.

His SDS background was not wasted as Grant admitted to assessing the political climate. He knew that offering the proposed program of services to persons with AIDS would be costly on many levels. It was not always simple to "do the right thing," or as he stated, "to witness and minister the Gospel in the difficult times." In the end, parishioners decided to move forward and provide the services, which did in fact cost them the financial support of some congregants. Some left the church and attended other parishes. Yet the program thrived, and surprisingly with a great deal of support from many of the older people within the congregation. One elderly volunteer religiously brought a copy of The New York Times. In one corner of the parish hall he led a discussion group selecting topics from the daily newspaper. Other volunteers, one a trained chef for a well-known actor, regularly prepared food.

So while conflicts surfaced throughout the decision-making process, and while there were open signs of hostility, new members and supporters also emerged. Ultimately the program thrived and served a clear purpose. In addition to a variety of social services, as Grant said, "for two years running we buried two people a month through that church —people who did not have any other place from which to say good-bye to this earthly existence."

While Grant did not mention having any close gay friends, he did discuss personal experiences that caused him to empathize with those in the gay community. He also shared his view that the inclusion of openly gay persons in the life of the church was a major event worth chronicling.

Loretta
Twenty years of ministry, University of the South/Sewanee, Tennessee

Loretta's path to priesthood included a series of twists and turns that took her across the United States, to England, and back. Prior to becoming an Episcopal priest, she had served as a deacon in the Anglican Church. She had also served as a nun. In spite of the challenges she encountered along the way, Loretta, now in her fifties, spoke of her experiences with the calm resolution of one who had in fact grown up in Berkeley, California, during the 1960s.

Loretta discussed a period in which she faced many conflicts both large and small. Some arose out of secrecy surrounding gay identities within the Church. Having spent a number of years in the Church of England, she observed:

> There is a very misogynistic queer community there. And it's like everybody knows it . . . and a standard joke among the clergy was that if every gay priest turned green tomorrow, what a colorful church it would be. And the fact is that there is one seminary in particular, St. Stephen's Church in Oxford, where basically you can't survive if you're a straight man.

Loretta shared her grueling experiences in an environment she described as misogynistic and interestingly enough, exceedingly progay. Raised in Berkeley with many gay friends, she found the environment in England surprising and disturbing on many levels. While serving as an ordained deacon, she found it necessary to carve out a support system to help her through the conflicts she experienced on a seemingly daily basis. She also admitted:

> I didn't fully negotiate it. I chose to leave England. . . . I think I am a better priest and person for having done it. I think it would have killed me psychologically to have stayed in that any longer.

In discussing her time serving as a deacon, she shared one especially memorable example that captured the depth of her frustration. Her rector was very adamant that she never relinquish the chalice during Communion—in spite of the protestations of the male clergy she would encounter. Apparently, a number of them so resented the presence of women in the role of deacon, they would not allow them to keep possession of the chalice during services. Loretta recalled an incident one Sunday as a physical struggle ensued when a visiting priest attempted to wrestle the cup away from her. Remembering her rector's words, she held on. Frustrated, but not to be outdone by a woman, the visiting priest bit her hand and finally took possession of the cup.

So Loretta's overseas experience left her physically as well as emotionally bruised. Yet in spite of the stress and the confrontations with closeted misogynistic gay priests in England, she maintained her resolve. Loretta said she was convinced by these experiences that the church needed to focus on inclusion rather than exclusion. From her perspective the closeted, aberrant, and bad behavior she experienced firsthand in England, and also observed in the United States, grew directly out of the exclusionary policies of the church.

Fiona
Ten years of ministry, Drew University

As a priest in her forties, Fiona's experiences concerning conflicts over gay inclusion within the Episcopal Church were marked by dramatic shifts. Some experiences were especially heart wrenching, while others seemed grounded in love. Regardless of the way in which the pendulum moved, for her the debate was always deeply personal. Though unequivocally supportive of gay rights, she has resisted the label of "gay priest." What was most surprising to me, however, was her tone. She was much more conciliatory than some of the straight clergy are toward those members of the church who are in opposition to gay rights. Yet, as a lesbian who elected to keep her sexual orientation private at the time of her ordination, she experienced conflicts on a very personal level.

She confessed that the early years of her ministry in the Episcopal Church resembled a roller coaster. For her these life-altering events included the 2006 Resolution to cease ordinations of openly gay and lesbian priests, as well as a subsequent overturning of this Resolution in 2009. Fiona likened the experience to a

> very large, awkward coming out process . . . where we've listened to uncles saying just horrible things. But it also feels like we've gone through a process of healing. And I feel like I have learned about the church that we really do sometimes need to take two steps backwards and then

three steps forward. And that's just the way we work. So it's been an awkward, but sort of a wonderful process.

Having weathered both large- and small-scale conflicts related to homosexuality, Fiona still emphasized the ties that bind. She relayed an experience she had in a bar in Columbus, Ohio, with a priest from the Diocese of Dallas, Texas. Their conversation revealed the very contradictions within the Episcopal Church that she and others have learned to embrace. As they chatted, they discovered that he knew the priest who baptized her. They also shared other bonds as Texans. Yet, as it turned out, he had been one of the leaders who had worked to keep gays from being ordained in the Episcopal Church.

The contradictions were unequivocal. They clearly enjoyed one another's company and felt a genuine connection as they laughed and discussed the best and worst places to find enchiladas outside of Texas. Yet at one point she felt compelled to let him know they were on *very* opposites sides when it came to the rights of gays within the Church. He calmly responded by saying, "Oh darlin' that's what happens in families: people get on different sides." The key sentiment for her was the importance of holding onto the idea of family, of continuing to be in relationship in spite of obvious differences of opinion.

Harry
Twenty years of ministry, Virginia Theological Seminary

Harry, an amiable priest in his forties with a calm, laid-back demeanor, grew up in a relatively conservative suburban neighborhood not far from his current parish. He also works part-time as a gym teacher at a local school. The daily camaraderie he found within his part-time profession has been especially welcomed as he admitted to feeling isolated at times as a priest. He greeted me warmly, waving from the top of a picture-perfect suburban landscape where one might not expect to be meeting with an advocate for gay rights. He had served on the Board of Oasis, a ministry that works for gay men and lesbians. He indicated that his circle of friends included gays who were "more together" than some of his heterosexual friends. He attributed this to the many personal challenges they had been through.

In his parish a controversy erupted following a special blessing in which he invited all the congregants to join him at the altar to bless a seminarian who had concluded a one-year visit at their church. During that time she was very involved in church activities and had preached on occasion. One sermon, in particular, alienated some parishioners when she referred to herself as a "dyke." In the open forums held to address the tensions that subsequently arose, there were verbal attacks by some of the elderly congregants. In one instance a widower said that he felt the seminarian, who was in a committed relationship, served to tarnish his relationship with his wife. He told the group, "It seems to cheapen what I had with my wife for the fifty years that we were married. What does that say about our marriage?" Harry tried to reassure the congregant by focusing on the common aspect of love. This he said helped the parishioner begin to think about the conflict in a new way.

Another elderly parishioner was much more heated in his attack. His graphic discussion of what he deemed the physical incompatibilities of same sex unions was concluded by his declaration that the "plumbing" just didn't fit. All this occurred in a small group setting originally designed to bring disagreeing parties together and provide all with a voice. In retrospect Harry admitted to regretting offering such completely open-ended discussions. There should have been tighter parameters, he said, as the comments, aimed directly at gay parishioners within the group, were just plain hurtful.

Full of vitriol and frustration, the man eventually returned to the Roman Catholic Church in which he had been raised. Yet despite their clear differences I was surprised to learn that he and Harry remain in contact. In fact, Harry had visited this very same parishioner in the hospital the previous day. He has also continued to perform baptisms for this former parishioner's grandchildren.

Greta
Twenty-two years of ministry, Union Theological Seminary

Greta was poised and charming and her surroundings seemed to reflect the grace and sensibilities of a bygone era. Yet the Tiffany grandfather clock in the corner of her living room and the traditional *Liberty*-like prints that adorned her home were in contrast to the complex set of experiences that she revealed concerning her personal conflicts over homosexuality. She had only served as a priest for twenty-two of her seventy-plus years. She attended seminary as a middle-aged woman who had raised three children.

The ongoing conflict she discussed was now resolved, but had directly involved one of her children. Greta's daughter did not come out to her mother until she was thirty-seven years old and had been married for many years. In addition to the inner conflict she experienced in fully accepting her daughter's sexual orientation, Greta also experienced a series of conflicts with the church that shifted as she evolved in her thinking.

She had not completely embraced the idea of full equivalency for same-sex marriage until the day of her daughter's commitment ceremony. She had agreed to officiate, but in 2003 was required to obtain permission from her bishop in advance. The bishop granted permission the night before the ceremony; however, she said that she would have officiated nonetheless.

> I would have had to have gone ahead. It would have broken my daughter's heart. I had nothing at stake. . . . They weren't going to excommunicate me or defrock me or something.

While she laughed at the notion of being defrocked, her definitive stance was in stark contrast to her earlier more clinical and conservative views. At one time she had been almost dismissive of her daughter's choices, thinking she would grow out of them. She had even chastised her daughter, but as she developed genuine friendships with gay men and women, her feelings softened. In fact, she said she believed God placed certain experiences and relationships in her life to enable her to become more accepting of her daughter's identity.

Her first experience reconciling the clash between her traditional view and an alternative one came when the son of her best friend disclosed his homosexuality to her exclusively. He said he approached her because he felt unable to tell his own mother. Though Greta described his personal family experience as "a long sad story," she also revealed that "my first feeling was, my goodness, this young man trusts me with this deep, dark secret of his." This and similar experiences contributed to a slow evolution of her views. As she said, "When I could totally accept a child of mine being that different, yes, it widened my spiritual self and my personal self."

Her transformation was so complete that for many years she joyfully gave presentations to other parents struggling to accept their children's gay identity. She spoke at churches and other gatherings, proudly sharing pictures of her daughter's commitment ceremony. Although in recent years she admitted that with a new generation the expectations had begun to shift and there was less of a need for her talks and reassuring messages to worried parents. She believed many—not all, but many—fears had diminished in the heterosexual contexts in which she had previously been asked to speak.

Ellen
Nine-and-a-half years of ministry, Connecticut Diocese School

Ellen came to ministry by way of a marketing career. She also served as a hospital administrator and was accustomed to dealing with assorted emergencies. In fact, our interview was interrupted briefly as she paused to take a call concerning a problem at the hospital. Yet she projected a very calm, wise, reasoned, and unflappable demeanor. I was taken aback when she admitted to having led what she deemed "a very adventuresome life." I was tempted to ask precisely what she meant by "adventuresome," but, as if reading my mind and not wanting to go there, she quickly began to speak about political upheavals of the 1960s. Now in her sixties, she had come of age in the South and observed the African-American Civil Rights Movement up close and personal. These experiences had shaped her significantly as she was filled with a strong sense of social justice.

She discussed a conflict that involved the church's support of those in their community with AIDS. In that time, the disease was viewed by her parish as a "homosexual issue." This was especially true for members of Ellen's parish from the West Indian community. Initially many vehemently opposed offering AIDS-related programs, fearing that their church would be labeled a "gay church." She attributed the success that she and her senior priest had experienced in resolving the conflict to their focus on love. "That's the thing that binds us all together." Ellen laughed and said that in her experience, the "What would Jesus do?" question helped to refocus the attention of those having the conflict.

> I would sit that question right down in the middle of the chicken fight, or the dogfight, or whatever it is we're having problems about. I would stick that right down in the middle of it and ask that question: So how would Jesus deal with this?

Compassion, in her view, was directly tied to identification with Jesus. She believed that the peace provided through his love enabled us to further advance peace.

Osmond

Over thirty-five years of ministry, General Theological Seminary

Tall, energetic, and looking very much like a Hollywood version of an English vicar, Osmond came bounding into the room. Now in his sixties, he had followed and admired Sloan Coffin, the former Yale Chaplain, senior minister of the Riverside Church in New York City, and well-known activist. Osmond laughed as he shared a quote he attributed to Coffin:

> He said that clergy are a lot like manure. If you spread them out across the fields, they have some usefulness. Bring them together in a pile, it's another thing altogether.

A sense of purposefulness and a desire to be useful resonated throughout the interview with Osmond. One of the parish conflicts he described stemmed from one individual's discomfort with homeless gay men in need of assistance. Elements of Osmond's personal conflicts with basic Christian understandings emerged as well. "I think the Puritan thing is one of several moments . . . of the Church doing an inadequate job of embracing our physicality." He thought that the Church was to blame for a preadolescent perspective on "human flesh." In his view, historically the Church has failed to provide an accurate understanding to the majority of Christians that their bodies are also part of God's creation.

> The early Church had a wacko (I suspect he was Republican) named Mani. He gave birth to a very helpful heresy called Manichaeism. It said creation was evil. You know, wives and husbands should cohabitate like brothers and sisters. And he also took scissors to the Scriptures and cut out things he didn't like. The point is the Church condemned Mani, and Manichaeism, and said Creation was good.

Yet Osmond does not think that this message has been shared sufficiently nor has it been emphasized by the Church. He suggested that a general Christian inability to discuss aspects of *hetero*sexuality comfortably makes us ill prepared to deal with homosexuality. Or as he put it, "To begin with, we're not really swinging at the ball from home plate. We're still in the dugout."

Connie

Seven years of ministry, Virginia Theological Seminary

Connie did not appear to be in her fifties. She seemed much younger and greeted me with the enthusiasm of an Evangelical. As it turned out she had, in fact, at one time been part of a very conservative Evangelical movement. The conflicts she had experienced in her current parish touched on issues of ethnicity and class, not sexuality. However, in her previous parish and in her personal life, she experienced conflicts that dealt directly with homosexuality and gay rights.

With exposure to contrasting viewpoints and as her own views became increasingly liberal, she felt a strain in her relationship with conservative family members who did not share her new perspective. Part of her personal evolution began in seminary. Her study of the Scriptures, and meeting gays and lesbians who were as deeply devoted in their faith and love of God as she was, were key factors that led to her change in thinking. She had also seen firsthand how the mere existence of gays within a local parish led to volatile expressions and actions that represented the antithesis of what she understood as Christianity. The revelation that a youth minister in her former church in Virginia was gay brought out the worst in parishioners. Having witnessed the carnage that resulted from emotional outbursts, she was convinced that, while there was a need for open discussions, they needed to be held within safe boundaries. Her experience in Virginia had been quite sobering.

> They didn't know he was gay and when they found out, you'd a thought they were going to hang him. I mean the most "spiritual" biblically literate leader of the church was the most outspoken ugly person I've ever heard . . . and I heard these stories of these young people who were absolutely traumatized because they loved this guy. And for the young people they didn't care if he was gay or straight. It didn't matter to them. But to hear this woman be so vitriolic. . . .

While she spoke freely of her own evolution, Connie's effervescent demeanor changed as she paused and told me that the subject of homosexuality was one she could approach only gingerly with family members. She said that her sister "has a very deep faith" and belongs to a conservative congregation in South Carolina that is on the verge of seceding from the Episcopal Church over national church efforts to be more inclusive of gays. While she and her sister have always been very close, the issue has torn at their relationship. She admitted that her sister expressed difficulty in understanding how she, Connie, evolved in her thinking. In recounting a conversation they had, Connie said her sister began by saying: "I just don't understand how you got from where you were to where you are."

> And we took about a three-hour walk and I began to just share. . . . It comes out of study and it comes out of relationships. . . . I think, I feel like I have a very keen sense of God's Holy Spirit at work in my own life and in the work of the Church. So when I hear the Holy Spirit at work in someone, I have to listen to that.

When asked how she negotiates her way through the conflict with her sister and her brother who is even more conservative, she said it resembles a dance. They come together about some things and then they go apart. Yet somehow they manage to stay in relationship. She laughed as she candidly admitted:

> We may not agree on this, but we'll give it a little more time. I want to say: "You stupid people, how can you. . . . If you listen to God's Spirit, how can you. . . ." But I say I know that my brother and sister, they love God with all of their hearts and that we're at very different places right now. It helps me get a lens that there are other Christians in the Church who feel very strongly and are trying to be faithful and we disagree.

Kelly
Eighteen years of ministry, Virginia Theological Seminary

Kelly is in her fifties and a passionate gardener. She told me that what appeals to her most about working in her garden is the freedom she experiences. In contrast, she is not entirely comfortable with the church's acceptance of homosexuality. In fact, when I read her the Conflict Scenario (see page 6), with which I started each interview, she admitted that such a scenario represented her worst nightmare. She struggles in part because she does not share the liberal views and policies of the diocese in which she serves. At times her speech was halting and she was almost apologetic as she shared her views. I imagined her on the defensive in gatherings within her diocese, which is known for its particularly liberal stance. By her own accounting she is not in full agreement with the church's position on homosexuality. Thus her personal struggle has been ongoing.

In addition, Kelly said she believed the Gospel's call for social justice required us to reach far beyond gay issues within the church. Her greater concerns were for finding ways to address hunger and poverty in sub-Saharan Africa, for example. Her frustrations stemmed from the myopic focus of gay supporters who overlooked what she viewed as larger social issues. Within her diocese, Kelly said that she and the minority who were even more conservative in their views felt ostracized and at times dismissed by the majority.

She explained that part of her evolution as a priest who had to resolve conflicts within her parish had involved compromise. At one time an admittedly ardent feminist, she indicated that she had learned to "tone that down." While she, for example, found gendered language problematic, Kelly indicated that she had learned to be more accommodating. She took into consideration those parishioners with a more traditional view whom she might alienate. While she might have preferred referring to God as female, she tempered this. As she said,

> I have to balance that with all the people that I'm going to totally offend. . . . I will sacrifice this part of me in order to try to be all things to all people. I can't be, but because I really believe that God loves everybody, and I don't think God wants A, B, and C to leave the church because I'm a feminist, I can tone down.

If it meant always referring to God as a man, she could do that rather than alienate conservative parishioners. From Kelly's perspective, the Episcopal Church has not been similarly accommodating with regard to those with conservative opinions. In her view the politics of the day overshadow the social justice issues that focus on the poor, the death penalty, and foreign aid. For Kelly the focus of the Episcopal Church on gay rights was problematic as it served to diminish the importance of other issues. "It's a piece of the Gospel, but I think we miss the whole thing when we focus on one piece at a time."

Connor
Thirty-five years of ministry, Lutheran Theological Seminary at Gettysburg

Connor had the roll-up-your-sleeves aura of an urban minister. In his sixties and having served as a priest for more than half of his life, he had negotiated many difficult conflicts over the course of his career, but he discussed them with a calm resolution. Many of those that took place within his parish were in some way related to efforts to extend rights, acceptance, and ultimately love to those within the gay community. In 1989, his parish hosted a gay and lesbian ministry, started by the diocese. Not everyone embraced the efforts to make the church more welcoming to both a gay and straight population. Some parishioners objected to the use of space by a group of self-proclaimed "dykes" as it brought negative attention to the church, but the vestry ultimately approved the ministry.

As he discussed these episodes two themes continued to surface—dialogue and direction.

> I do think you have to open lines of communication and I do think you have to talk about where your church stands. Not just your local church, but your denomination in all of this. And then you have to work out what is your pathway.

The communication efforts ultimately served to engender support. By parishioners listening to one another expressing the deeper hopes, fears, joys, and sorrows, connections grew and eventually deepened. Though some people left, new members joined and long-time parishioners became engaged in new ways. They struggled to move from what had been a dying church to a growing church. As Connor recounted, one day as he was in the midst of pushing for change and inclusion, a widowed parishioner in her seventies addressed the church. It was Pentecost Sunday and he said this long-time member had the audacity to stand up and say:

> I don't know what Connor's doing. And frankly, I don't care anymore because he's brought the children back to the church. And I want to go to church where there's children under my feet. So whatever he's doing, I'm going to do it with him. Cause I want the children back.

While the conflicts Connor and the congregation faced together were at times huge, he said he believed "that was what I was called to do. I got beaten up, but I knew that was where I was supposed to go." For priests especially he believed that it was very important that at the end of the day they be able to engage in a prayer life and understand that they were doing what they were genuinely called to do. He said:

I just felt that somehow from the time I was born I was called to be an urban priest. I always felt that I was called to do this.

Petra
Eighteen years of ministry, Yale Divinity School

For Petra, a priest in her forties, conflicts over gay rights presented challenges in the personal, parish, and national arenas. For her, gay rights were without question very much of a social justice issue. She hoped she would be as resolute in her beliefs and as committed to the issue even if her father had not been gay. In a previous parish she had been involved in negotiating conflicts with several conservative members who were very angry because of the evolving corporate views of the Episcopal Church. The ordination of the first openly gay bishop sent them over the edge and they began an e-mail vent aimed at Petra and the rector that lasted for many months. The couple's rant and their desire to exclude others from full participation in the church stood in direct contrast to Petra's firm belief in the inclusive nature of the church. For her, it was quite simple:

> Spiritual matters are matters of expansion rather than contraction. Any spirituality and faith tradition shouldn't be about defining who isn't one of us, but rather how we can embrace.

And yet in the conflicts she had faced, she also indicated that there were occasions when it was ultimately necessary to part ways. So she was at times challenged to balance these two seemingly contradictory expectations—inclusion and a parting of the ways. This need to balance contradictions was also evident as she spoke of the larger national church issues in relation to the Anglican Communion. In the end she said:

> If you love the church, have been ordained as a spokesperson for the church, . . . eventually you're going to have to work within the structures of the church, change the structures, or leave. But don't stay and make it so hard for everyone else to get on with the business of what they need to do. If I have resentment around this particular issue, it's that. It's the people who don't break off but stay and take all the resources—financial, emotional, spiritual

resources that could be used to address any number of problems that are really huge in the world right now.

From her perspective the polity of the church needed to be respected. Following many heartfelt conversations within the church, she said it was now important to move forward and carry on with the essential business of the church.

Dennis
Fifty years of ministry, Episcopal Theological Seminary Southwest/Austin, Texas

Dennis was unequivocal in his support of gay and lesbian rights. At eight-four, he had served more years as a priest than most of the individuals I spoke with had lived. Feisty and passionate in his convictions, Dennis had admittedly weathered many stormy conflicts throughout the course of his ministry. Having grown up in Mississippi, he was also very sensitive to racial issues and their implications. He saw a direct link between the social justice issues of racial equality and the push for gay inclusion. An exchange with congregants over the depiction of the president of the United States reflected both his passions and his concerns.

In the fall of 2009 the *New York Post* included a controversial cartoon that some believed depicted President Obama as a chimpanzee. Dennis said he addressed what he believed were the negative implications of the cartoon in a sermon and expressed his own disappointment in the *Post*. In the midst of the service he heard one parishioner critique his comments. With a determined tone Dennis admitted, "So they were waiting for me and I was waiting for them." A discussion followed in the parish hall.

For Dennis the issue was more than a matter of racial politics. It was a matter of justice that had to be achieved whether it was for African-Americans in Mississippi or gays in New York City. The principle was the same. Issues of social justice required not only large-scale political actions, but also small, individual steps. He felt it was imperative that we speak out against injustices relating to racism or efforts to exclude gays:

> I don't know how much we individually can do, but we have to remember that it always starts from the bottom. It never starts from the top . . . but I think any time you see any injustice anywhere you have to speak. Even if you just speak to one person. But there again, if you can

get one person who's doing it to understand what you're talking about, I think you've accomplished a great deal.

Carole
Three-and-a-half years of ministry, Diocese Diaconal Formation Program

Carole was relatively new to ministry. Though in her fifties, she had only served as a deacon for three and a half years. Yet she was baptized and raised in the Episcopal Church. The experience of having a number of gay friends and having a husband whose family she described as both racist and homophobic sometimes made negotiating family life very much akin to walking a tightrope. The casual comments of family members were personally offensive to her, but she had to maintain a long-term relationship with all parties so she needed to tread carefully. Though exhausting at times, through patience she had made inroads. She said that her in-laws had in fact grown to love one of her best friends, who is gay and a godparent to her children.

Over the years she employed a strategy that involved focusing on the commonality of family experiences. Sharing holidays, birthdays, supporting one another through difficult times, bound them together and allowed them, much like Connie and her conservative sister, to gradually move toward hearing the other's point of view. Those bonds served as a bridge to help them across the more controversial moments. Patience did not come easily as Carole described her husband's relatives as a family of talkers. Or as she said, "They don't take a lot of breath." She told me that she attempts to be tolerant and nonconfrontational, and described herself as open to listening to other opinions whether she agrees with them or not:

> I don't believe that getting into a fight about these issues is helpful. I don't like to battle with people . . . and it doesn't further the relationship to shut things down. I mean, they are family.

And a family that has given her much practice in listening. The importance of "family" and "the community" surfaced as one of her genuine concerns. In fact, as an ordained deacon, her role includes bringing the cares and concerns of the world to the church and subsequently mobilizing the church to go out into the world and address those concerns. As deacon she is both reconciler and advocate and must balance these disparate roles.

Dean

Fifty years of ministry, Perkins School of Theology

Dean brought with him the peace of someone who had spent a lifetime reconciling differences and was comfortable in doing so. His strategies for success were developed during his youth and he later received formal training through workshops and through exposure to those engaged in conflict resolution. As he said, growing up in the South, "I did find that people begin to get used to an idea and then begin to accept it. But it can be very slow, painful, and agonizing."

Now in his seventies, Dean's efforts to bring dissimilar parties together began in his youth. He was very deliberate in his approach. He called the strategy he employed "gradual integration." Growing up in the South during the early stages of the African-American Civil Rights Movement, he had no shortage of opportunities to employ his gradual integration strategy. While he did not describe his parents as actively racist, he did say they were "traditionally Southern," which meant that socialization between those from different ethnic and social groups simply did not take place. Yet when Dean attended college, he was exposed to new customs and traditions. He developed friendships with individuals from many different cultural, social, ethnic, and national backgrounds.

Although it sounded a bit like a social experiment, his strategy was effective. When he came home on holidays throughout his college years, he brought a diverse group of friends with him. On the first occasion his friend had skin whiter than his, but he was Mexican. Though reluctant to have a Mexican visit, upon his arrival Dean's family was taken over by his warmth, charm, and skill as a musician. During the next holiday, he brought home another Mexican friend and this time his family was less resistant, having fully embraced his first friend. The second Mexican visitor, however, was much darker in complexion. He too came to be well received by his family. Following this pattern, Dean finally brought home a married African-American couple whom he described as wonderful. By this time his family had grown to accept the idea that social interactions with those from different ethnic backgrounds were not only possible, but also personally rewarding. His family grew to love and appreciate the African-American couple as well.

While Dean expressed a belief that individuals had to take the lead in addressing social injustices, Dean also saw that as the role of the Church. He envisioned a Church in which congregants and clergy applied their faith with boldness. He said he believed

[as] Martin Luther King said, the Church should be the headlight not the taillight of society. And I think the Church needs to be courageously open to the future. It should be a place where the marginalized and the hurting can find solace. We need a vision of the Church as the beloved community . . . that holds us together. It's too easy to just go to the church and go through ritual and think that we've worshiped. There's just so much hurting in the world. And the Church needs to share in that hurting. . . . Church is too often seen as a refuge. It is a refuge, but it also gives us our marching orders. And the two are in a creative tension.

Peter
Twelve years of ministry, Memphis Theological Seminary

Though he does not view himself as an activist, Peter did express the sentiment that simply being in the church and doing what he does every day is, in fact, political. Though he has served twelve years in the ministry without the benefit of formal conflict resolution training, Peter's discussion of conflict resolution resembled that of priests with many more years of experience and formal training. He also admitted that his expectations concerning conflicts had been shaped to some extent by his work in the commercial airline industry where he had seen a shift in the handling of passengers' "bad behavior." He had certainly been exposed to the good and less effective ways to manage conflict.

As a gay man in his forties, he had also had to negotiate any number of conflicts. Admittedly the most brutal one he ever negotiated took place at a church where he and his partner were parishioners. Peter was attending seminary at the time. They had always felt it was important to worship together. Peter was very open about their status as a couple as they searched for a congregational home. After being told by six parishes that they would not be welcome as worshipers, they finally found a church that was initially accepting.

Unfortunately for them, their rector, and the entire parish, acceptance unexpectedly changed to hostility when a Boy Scout liaison was needed. As an active participant in many other church activities, his partner volunteered. This led to an internal church battle that unearthed underlying tensions, permanently divided the church, and subsequently led to the rector's resignation and ultimately to the closing of the church.

Peter said that it was deconsecrated and a Walgreen's pharmacy was subsequently built on the land.

A member of the congregation was not in favor of a gay man serving as liaison to the Boy Scouts. The rector held a distinctly different and oppositional view. It was her belief that while the Boy Scouts had their policy, they could not dictate church policy or her policy. Parishioners took sides, and this set off an explosive series of events in which many came to resent the priest for making her decisions apart from the congregation. To make matters worse, Peter said she was also isolated from above, as her bishop was hostile toward homosexuals. In fact, he was the same bishop who told Peter, as he moved through the process of ordination, that he would never lay hands on him to thereby bless his ordination. Meanwhile, Peter's rector in her attempt to minimize escalating tensions eventually asked that he and his partner step aside from all nonworship activities within the church. Peter said that the climate had become so hostile that during the so-called "passing of the peace," some congregants simply refused to acknowledge him.

Though there were some supporters in the congregation, and while the rector had been well intentioned, Peter reported that it was a case study of what *not* to do when attempting to resolve conflicts. Not only was it difficult for him, but he indicated that the rector paid a high price as well. "I think it was just an incredibly painful, lonely place where she felt a lack of support . . . and was just painfully alone." He also described the series of events as if they represented a watershed moment. Certainly he had learned from the experience. Having developed a deep personal interest, he subsequently read a great deal on his own about practical strategies designed to help one manage conflicts effectively. As excruciatingly painful as the experience had been, it was equally instructive. It became a case of experiential learning that was viscerally carved into his memory.

Barclay
Twelve years of ministry, Church Divinity School of the Pacific

While Barclay laughingly described his diocese as residing somewhere to the left of Che Guevara, he has experienced no shortage of conflicts. He expressed great admiration for the Presiding Bishop who attended his seminary. His admiration in part seemed to stem from her ability to manage conflict and challenges to her authority with grace. In his fifties, openly gay and partnered, Barclay had been forced to negotiate conflicts within the church even before he was called to his current parish.

Though he was not their first choice, the parish in which he now serves reopened discussions with him after the selected candidate declined their offer. Initially Barclay was rejected because he was gay. He smiled and pointed out that he still is. Yet when members of the parish did an analysis of the qualities they sought most—wise, loving, dedicated, hard working—they recognized that he was the right choice for them irrespective of his sexual orientation.

He said that one of the major challenges for him as a rector is the lack of direct communication. Parishioners don't come to him directly. He said, "They will come to the corner and scream." The first time that happened, he screamed as well, but has since learned to handle situations more effectively by taking a much more centered approach. He has also taken his vestry through formal steps in order to better understand more effective approaches to conflict resolution. In addition, he indicated that he has a very supportive partner and an excellent spiritual director.

One of the chief difficulties he identified was the erosion of civility in both the Episcopal Church and the society-at-large. He said it was especially jarring within the church because Episcopalians used to be very civil; even when in dispute over serious concerns, they simply did not speak to one another in an abusive way.

In Conclusion

So there was no shortage of intricately woven and sometimes wrenching conflict experiences from which these clergy members could draw upon to reflect. While I was initially concerned that there might be some reluctance to voice criticisms of the Church or to speak candidly concerning controversial issues, surprisingly, this was not the case. There did not appear to be any self-imposed, muted response to any of the questions asked.

Clergy seemed genuinely interested in putting their past struggles to good use in order to help others improve in their efforts to resolve conflicts. Though none felt they had all the answers, they were willing to contribute so that others might avoid some of their mistakes. In addition to their understanding of current church conflicts, they brought their theological training and a willingness to reflect on complex issues.

Though their stories and experiences differ from one another, there was a consensus that it was impossible to avoid conflicts, whether it was in one's church, one's personal life, or within the larger society. As much as they may have disliked conflict encounters, there was simply no escape, and some brought a reluctant recognition that the only way out was through. Their experiences offer a sampling of the types of conflicts clergy are routinely called to resolve. Some are of a personal nature while others involve the entire parish. Though the conflicts differ, questions concerning faith emerge with regularity.

On the institutional level, conflicts relating to matters of faith and the sexual orientation of those within the Episcopal Church have in recent years gained much media attention. Comparatively little has focused on how clergy learn to resolve these conflicts on the personal and congregational levels. Yet learn they do, and often it is without the benefit of formal training. Some have engaged in a process of questioning not only themselves, but also their families, friends, and congregations, as they all struggle to make meaning in the midst of social change. Conversations with these members of the clergy, each deeply connected to the Episcopal Church, revealed a vibrant form of engagement and a process of learning guided by religious principles as well as an ability to manage complexity. So exactly how did these distinctly unique personalities cultivate a priestly attitude and manage complex conflict scenarios by adopting an arms out, palms open approach?

Questions to Ponder

1. What are the most difficult conflicts I have been called to resolve?

2. Did I handle all of these conflicts in a similar manner? Was there a pattern to my approach to resolving them?

3. In instances where I was able to successfully resolve the conflict, what were the most distinctive features of my approach?

4. How would I describe the general attitude I bring to conflict situations?

Part 2 | What They Learned

LERGY LEARNED THAT assuming the posture of a priest was a key to their success in negotiating conflicts. With arms out and palms open, one conveys empathy and love while at the same time one is able to establish personal balance. These dual responsibilities, to others and to oneself, surfaced as key elements in cultivating the priestly attitude that helped move conflict negotiations forward effectively. While initially it appears counterintuitive, it was with outstretched arms that clergy were able to make necessary adjustments, maintain an inner balance, and reach toward others to achieve reconciliation and resolution.

Clergy extended themselves in order to support those involved in the conflict and they also extended these supports to themselves. By this I mean they did not overlook the fact that they themselves were in need of nurturing. So they made sure they received the necessary support in order to proceed toward success. When they were most successful, they reached out from a place of love to support those in the conflict as they also embraced the support that they themselves required as negotiators in the midst of conflict. Both forms of outreach emerged as vital elements.

Maintaining the right balance between these equally important demands required very specific skills, which are enumerated in chapter 3. Clergy also devised broad strategies and developed an attitude that helped to create an environment that was conducive to the resolution of conflicts. These strategies and attitudes are the subject of chapter 2.

One of the major pieces of knowledge that clergy took away from their conflict experiences was the importance of extending outreach and support to the broadest circle of individuals affected by the conflict. Not just support for individuals, but also communal support was an important part of their resolution strategy. Clergy indicated that it was often through broad-based community involvement that they were most successful in creating a climate that was conducive to reaching a resolution.

CHAPTER 2

Strategies for Cultivating
a Priestly Attitude

The prevailing attitude conveyed by clergy was one of caring and support. An overwhelming majority indicated that they needed to include, and reach beyond, the aggrieved parties to provide a variety of supports for the entire community affected by the conflict during negotiations. The strategies designed to offer support took two very distinct paths. First, external support was offered to the community at large. This involved strengthening relationships within the church hierarchy and the general congregation. It also involved using the conflict to generate learning opportunities for the entire community.

Secondly, care and support were seen as vital elements for clergy themselves. There was a clear recognition that efforts to resolve highly emotional conflicts took a personal toll. They were only able to negotiate the conflict, and manage associated pressures designed to throw them off balance, when they were not consumed by the conflict. It became necessary to focus on other areas of importance. This included seeking out spiritual support for themselves. At times, however, there were simply inherent religious contradictions they were required to accept.

Fostering a Climate of Reconciliation

Perhaps the very first step in cultivating a priestly attitude included fostering a climate of reconciliation that led to resolution. Regardless of whether or not clergy had received formal conflict resolution training, the general tone of responses ran counter to what might be seen as natural inclinations. This tone was, however, grounded in love and thus in keeping with the most foundational of Christian principles. While they took advantage of their own mechanisms of support, clergy displayed an understanding that their personal needs could not outweigh the needs of others, and when necessary they balanced their own strong emotions with a sense of humility.

Balancing competing interests is an inherent part of a religious life. Even as they begin their careers, clergy are required to balance many dueling and worthy interests. It is a challenge for educators of clergy as well. Efforts to maintain a balance between opposing forces within a religious context surfaced not only with large-scale institutional issues but also in the many challenges that arose during conflict resolutions.

While it is easy to say clergy sought to allow love to overshadow any fears, the word *love* itself encompasses many dimensions and has many different meanings according to the context and according to individual understandings. What the men and women I interviewed conveyed as they recounted their experiences was very much akin to an *agape*, or a paternal, unconditional form of love. It was reflected in their concern for the broader community of those affected by the conflict that clergy were attempting to resolve.

At some point during negotiations, they were often called to convey the self-sacrificing aspect of this *agape* love. Being called to care for the souls of others was not a responsibility taken lightly. And perhaps that is what allowed them to remain or at least return to the inclusive posture of a priest. Yet what if I am not a priest? What are the actions and behaviors I can emulate in order to create a climate conducive to reconciliation?

Maintaining the right attitude involved more than a philosophy. It incorporated very specific strategies that can benefit disputants and negotiators alike regardless of their religious affiliations. At times the process involved taking oneself out of the equation. So, for example, clergy often deferred their own immediate needs. The emphasis was not on aggressively putting their personal agenda forward. Such aggression, as Peter observed his priest display in her conflict with the parish over his partner's offer to work with the Boy Scouts, did not generally lead to a positive outcome. Among those who were more successful, there was a much greater emphasis on nurturing the broad spectrum of individuals engaged in the conflict. Rather than muscling their way through conflict negotiations, it was much more as if they were attempting to love their way through the dispute. Yet such love was not a passive, undisciplined form of engagement. The love they brought to their interactions superseded a need for immediate approvals. So at times a "tough love" did exist.

And there was apparently enough love to go around. Clergy did not ignore their own personal needs, as will be discussed later in this chapter. Yet they first discussed attending to the emotional and spiritual wounds of others. While some struggled mightily to do this, they nonetheless understood that ultimately it was not about protecting their own position, but about a willingness to be vulnerable.

In the short-term, the greater good involved a resolution to the conflict. In taking a longer, spiritually oriented gaze, their concerns were much broader if not eternal. When they were able to seize upon these larger concerns, they were freed sufficiently to be able to focus less on being heard and more on actively listening. The general sentiment was that it was necessary to be open and more inclusive (to operate from a place of love) than it was to pull away and retrench (operate from a place of fear) even though the latter approach may have felt personally safer. It was with arms out and palms open that they were able to maintain their balance and move across the tightrope most effectively.

But what if I am not yet operating from that level of generosity? If one is able to shift one's perception slightly and understand that conflict has the potential to take us into new domains that offer unexpected advantages, it can be a little easier to release some of our fears and let go of our intransigence. Rather than frame our view of conflict as a tug-of-war-either-or proposition—where I win and you lose or vice versa—there is a third possibility.

We can elect to see conflict as something that provides us with the opportunity to enter a new domain that neither party had imagined. In this sort of triangulated view, we need not remain entrenched in our positions and at odds. Though conflict is often seen in terms of warfare, villains, and efforts to outstrategize or take advantage of "opponents," that is a very restrictive view. Instead it is possible to view it as an experience that has the potential to launch us into a better place. This occurs only to the extent we are willing to reach beyond immediate concerns and embrace conflict as an opportunity for communal, personal, or spiritual growth.

Clergy Members Needed
to Support the Community by . . .

Reaching Out to Key Congregants

While clergy faced a distinct set of institutional and emotional challenges along the way, a large majority utilized the community strategically, and an overwhelming majority offered targeted forms of support according to the individual needs of those involved in the conflict. Sustaining the community was most commonly demonstrated through different forms of outreach. Clergy described an approach that supported the community on a variety of fronts by reaching out to multiple constituents to address their needs throughout negotiations. The primary goal of all efforts was to maintain strong bonds and good relationships within the church. As Grant, a priest who brought nearly forty years of ministry to such encounters, expressed it:

> One of the things I'm clear about in terms of this vocation, and I'm sure about others, but in terms of this vocation specifically, is that this is all based on relationships. On our relationships with each other, our relationships with God, our relationships as a community, our relationships as an institution, but it's all based on relationships.

Various forms of support were utilized to build and to strengthen these relationships. As a result, clergy took on many roles, including that of mother, educator, negotiator, advocate, psychologist, confidant, and even that of child in need of nurturing. Forms of support for the community were not one-dimensional. Outreach to congregants was comprehensive and designed to address a variety of needs and preferences.

Clergy also expressed a belief that "tough love" was sometimes needed in order to support the community as a whole. So while collaborative outreach was deemed important, there were times when it was also necessary to take a clear, definitive, and sometimes unpopular stand. In discussing his approach, Barclay, a priest who had weathered many conflicts and seen his own resolution skills improve over time, talked of experiences with his current congregation:

> They said they wanted a collaborative leader . . . but initially that meant that we couldn't make any decisions. Anyone could make any decision and it could be vetoed at any time.

Clearly this was not the most effective approach. In this instance in order to be successful, he said he was forced to adopt a much more authoritarian stance. Others echoed this sentiment and discussed how they had struggled to achieve the right balance. While they sought to reach out to key congregants in a collaborative manner, they learned through experience that they could not simply relinquish their role as leaders of the congregation.

Yet they also designed strategies that incorporated the structural expectations of the church. This is not surprising, as it is a structured denomination. As Peter pointed out:

> In the Episcopal Church we are governed somewhat by what our bishop allows us to do and not do, and there is a particular hierarchy that we follow. So if you're an Episcopal priest in an Episcopal congregation, there's a certain ethos of being part of the Worldwide Anglican Communion in the way we run things.

In the church in which he worshiped as a seminarian—the church that was deconsecrated following a conflict generated by his partner's offer to help a Boy Scout group—the rector had neglected to successfully incorporate members of the parish in efforts to resolve the problem. In instances where the conflict involved the parish, ideally outreach included the congregation-at-large, but the reach also extended to those who were a part of the church hierarchy. A majority of the priests I spoke with specifically stated that they would work within the Episcopal hierarchy to resolve the conflict. In responding to the Conflict Scenario (see page 6) that was read at the start of each interview, common responses included: "I would present the situation to the wardens." "I would work first through the leadership which is our rector of wardens and vestry." "I'd talk with the wardens." "I'd look at the vestry."

The first inclination to resolve the conflict was one that was mindful of the church hierarchy. Even as they had their own vision of where they needed to be, they were respectful of the institutional structures in place. Even Loretta, with her laid-back Berkeley upbringing, commented:

> We are in a structured church. And the priest acting like the Lone Ranger is usually a nonstarter. That's how you alienate congregations.

Clergy also overwhelmingly indicated that their approach to the conflict would require them to balance their views with, or incorporate their views into, a process of discovery that would include the entire congregation. It was not uncommon for clergy to outline a systematic approach that resembled the one outlined by Grant in response to the Conflict Scenario. His strategy incorporated the formal and informal hierarchy of wardens, mentors, leaders, and advisors. Grant said he felt it was important to approach them even prior to discussions with the congregation-at-large:

> So I would start with the wardens. I would certainly move to discuss things with what I would call my advisors. Some would be mentors. . . . The next piece I think in an ideal process would be to identify the leaders in the people who were angry or hurt, and I would schedule one-on-one interviews with them and after that I would restart the cycle. I would come back to the wardens. I would come back to my advisors and say this is what I've learned.

Those who were within the formal church hierarchy, including wardens and the vestry, as well as those who were part of unofficial hierarchies, were encouraged to collaborate in efforts to resolve the conflict. Thus both informal and formal social networks were utilized.

Strengthening Relationships

The strengthening of relationships over time was emphasized as being part of an effective strategy by more than half of clergy. Carole, a deacon who experienced a long-term conflict with her in-laws concerning their views on homosexuality, found that other elements of family life held them together in ways that superseded the conflict. Her two best friends were not people who would normally be included within her in-laws' circle of friends. One was born with characteristics of both sexes (intersex) and was assigned a female gender. Her other best friend from childhood is a gay man. He and his partner of thirty years are godparents to her children. She described her husband's family as both racist and homophobic. A variety of related conflicts have emerged over the years. Yet progress has been made with ongoing exposure and her concerted efforts to stay in relationship with her in-laws in spite of their differences. Now Carole admitted, "Over these thirty years, they do know someone who is gay. . . . And they've grown to love him."

Maintaining connections with these family members served to sustain the relationships despite moments of conflict. Tensions were resolved over time as she allowed the relational aspects of family life to take precedence over the conflict itself.

Others described this very same pattern of interaction in relation to conflicts within a parish. The importance of maintaining bonds and reaching out consistently was underscored. In response to the Conflict Scenario, one priest with eighteen years of ministry who currently serves as rector of a pastoral-sized parish, which generally includes parishes with approximately one hundred worshipers each Sunday, offered a comprehensive approach that focused on strengthening relationships. Petra's approach was echoed by many others:

> I would build on existing relationships. I would have some conversations individually with the people who had come to me to express their discontent. I would express support for the couple. I would look at what's allowed within the polity of my particular denomination . . . and then after that I would put it out for the congregation with the permission of the couple. I would be very open. . . . Because I do believe the truth sets you free. . . . And I really do believe in bringing everyone together in conversation.

One priest, who for many years resisted being identified by her sexual orientation, now serves in a traditionally conservative parish. She found that building individual relationships and deepening those bonds with parishioners led to acceptance over time. For Fiona, the way to resolve conflicts relating to the acceptance of gays is always through relationships. She emphasized the need to establish ties and laughed heartily as she described the ironic point of agreement she shared with members of her congregation at the outset.

> It's got to be personal relationships. No one at my church wanted to call a "gay priest" and they probably called me because I really didn't even want to be a "gay priest." So we had this in common. But through the relationships that we've developed, people are now even actively saying our next priest should be a gay priest too, 'cause they seem to be the best. If you're able to stay in relationship with people over time, that's really what convinces people.

This process of strengthening relationships also included outreach to the most disaffected members of the community, especially during the most difficult moments of the conflict. It was viewed as extremely important that they be given a voice and allowed to vent. Yet there were occasions when such allowances proved to be difficult.

Several priests emphasized the need for establishing clear and safe boundaries. In response to a conflict that developed out of a series of events following a sermon in which a visiting lesbian seminarian referred to herself as a "dyke," Harry held several adult forums and small group discussions. One of the most disaffected of the group became vicious in his attack, stating that homosexuality was wrong, that the "plumbing" just doesn't fit. Looking back at the experience, Harry said of his efforts:

> I wanted to let him and everybody feel like they could speak their mind, but . . . his comments were totally inappropriate and not helpful to the discussion.

Subsequent to this outburst, the disgruntled congregant returned to the Roman Catholic Church in which he had been raised. Yet even as this relationship was strained because of his outburst, others were deepened and new relationships were formed. Harry said that the lashing out was so hurtful that other members of the congregation stepped forward to offer their support to gay parishioners who were the target of the attack. In instances where it was anticipated that emotions might escalate, other formats were deemed preferable. Petra, for example, said, "I would have some conversations individually with the people who had come to me to express their discontent." Similarly, Fiona said that in her experience a performance element sometimes entered the discussions when the conversation took place in larger formats. Fiona said that in the quiet of one-on-one conversations, a much different tone was taken. She observed:

> In public discourse people tend to be very abrasive and sort of confrontational. But in private people tend to be pretty gentle with one another.

The effort to be gentle in ushering congregants through the conflict was cited by some clergy members as necessary. Yet it was only one of many strategies sited as being important.

Educational Support

Over half of those who discussed educational efforts were passionate about the role it played in bringing about a reconciliation especially with regard to efforts to be more inclusive of gays within the church. A variety of forms of educational programming helped to support the community as they worked toward a resolution. Learning experiences were provided through educational offerings that could be very structured, open-ended, or even covert. The introduction of an AIDS program caused dissent in yet another congregation during the height of the epidemic. Ellen, a priest with a marketing background, recalled her experience with an extremely conservative woman in her thirties who was an informal leader within the church. Ellen said the woman was vehemently opposed to the program.

> She was angry about this. Very, very angry about us providing this AIDS ministry. She didn't think it was appropriate. And the guy that I served with and I continued to try to bring her to be a part of it. Well, not a part of it literally, but in being more involved in the church. We made her a reader in the church. Now if you're going to stand up in front of people and you're reading the Gospel . . .

Ellen laughed as she recalled the success of this strategy. In the end it became difficult for the parishioner to read out loud on a weekly basis about the love of God and continue to direct her hostilities toward the AIDS ministry, which was strategically named the Ministry of Love.

Of those who felt an educational offering of some kind was in order, it was often provided as an important counterbalance to misinformation that was generally available and reinforced. Osmond took a practical approach, but one that was grounded in intellectual and scriptural understandings. He believed that Christianity, the Episcopal Church, and most especially the Roman Catholic Church had not served Christians well with regard to their general understanding of sexuality. He expressed his concern that the Church had done an inadequate job of embracing our physicality as humans.

To counter widespread misconceptions, he suggested that offering a course on the church and sexuality was vital. So many Christians, in his opinion, lacked accurate information. Members of the Episcopal Church were simply not trained to discuss the human body. Roman Catholics, he thought, while they received much media attention, were even less prepared to do so. Concerning the majority of Christians, he said:

All they know is that the Pope's hot list of red-button issues are all body issues—women and holy orders, homosexuality, abortion, contraception.

In his efforts to work toward a resolution, Osmond said he would make an effort to surround the congregation with a comprehensive set of educational offerings. The focus on education was, like other strategies used to resolve the conflict, multifaceted. In some cases, a high-level intellectual discourse was in order. For others, a more fundamental discussion was required. Some brought their educational efforts to an even wider audience beyond the congregation. Fiona, who is openly gay, regularly teaches a course at a local Catholic college.

> I always begin my lecture on homosexuality and the Bible with my lecture on slavery and the Bible. 'Cause I can prove to you that slavery is ok. I can show you the passages where it's okay, Old and New Testament. . . . Yet there's absolutely no one left in the world who believes that slavery's good. . . . We're just supposed to look at that and think that's a situation of their time. . . . I think in the same way it's going to be really quick that we get to that place with homosexuality.

In the smorgasbord of educational offerings discussed by clergy, there was a real effort to meet congregants where they were. Informal coffee hours, Lenten short courses, workshops, guest speakers, small group adult forums, and Bible study were all mentioned as possible vehicles for educating parishioners, depending upon the needs of the community. And apparently, one could make no assumptions. One priest recounted his experience with a pillar of the parish who revolted following the opening of a soup kitchen, shelter, and AIDS hospice. No one was more surprised than Osmond when this man,

> following Wednesday 10 a.m. mass, . . . came back to the parish house. The street people were beginning to collect for lunch and he yells: "Kick these bums out of here!" And so I said, "Can I talk to you?" . . . So that afternoon I went to his apartment and asked, "Let me show you in the Bible where this sort of all comes from." He did not own a Bible! He was in his seventies, maybe eighties. So I realized I'm up against enormous ignorance here.

In this case and others, education and communal supports helped to soften resistance. This angry parishioner did eventually accept the idea of offering support to those with AIDS who came to the hospice and homeless shelter. Osmond said that it was actually this man's social network within the church that played an important role here. Peers from his parish helped educate and usher him through the process of reconciliation. Practical efforts on Osmond's part included scheduling changes whereby the homeless groups' and the morning worshipers' paths did not cross. This served to ease tensions as well.

Throughout the educational process, which was aimed at bringing resolution to the conflict, clergy strove to remain centered and not lose track of their ultimate priorities. They stressed the importance of finding a way to maintain a sense of community and to coexist. As Dennis, who brought fifty years of pastoral experience, put it:

> No matter how I feel about the people involved, I try to remember this is part of God's creation too. I try to, but I don't always succeed in the heat of it. But that's why I try to back off and to say look, we have to learn to live together. And I try to take that approach.

Yet at times this required a great deal of effort. For many conflict negotiators, the outbursts, such as the one exhibited by the parishioner who wanted the homeless kicked out of his church, proved to be a very draining experience.

Clergy Members Needed to Support Themselves by . . .

Understanding the Personal Toll on Clergy / Seeking Emotional Support

In describing those strategies that led to resolutions, support for the community was deemed important, but self-care was deemed necessary as well. More than half of the individuals I spoke with acknowledged that emotional support for clergy was vital. There was a clear recognition that conflict negotiations had the potential to wear down the negotiators, especially those balancing as many responsibilities as clergy were required to balance. As much as they were concerned about their parishioners and as much as they worked diligently to lead with compassion, it was apparent from their direct and indirect responses that they too were in need of nurturing.

Negotiating these emotional conflicts were reported as taking a significant toll on the majority of clergy and for some, negotiating proved to be a very painful experience. While slightly over half of the clergy expressed a concern that the conflict might cause parishioners to leave the church, only three expressed a concern over decreased pledges and a corresponding decrease in financial support. What *was* associated with the loss of parishioners, however, was pain. While potential financial losses did not prevent them from taking what they deemed to be the appropriate steps to resolve conflicts, clergy did indicate that the loss of even one parishioner was deeply personal and could be excruciating. Losing members of the flock they were charged to care for was not a loss taken lightly. It resembled and in fact was experienced as the loss of a loved one. So even while Harry deemed one parishioner's verbal abuse of gays within the parish totally inappropriate, when the man left to attend another church Harry nonetheless admitted, "It broke my heart when George left."

Similar language was used to describe the potential loss of a same-sex couple forced to leave the church because of sentiments from other parishioners. If the couple was not comfortable in her parish or said it was not a place we feel at home and left, Petra said she would be heartbroken. Similar sentiments were expressed, almost verbatim by Connie. She said that if efforts to reach a viable resolution for all parties concerning their commitment ceremony failed, she would be heartbroken if she was forced to say, "I'm sorry—I'll have to find you another church. You know we can't do it here—there's too much dissention."

While the pain experienced by some clergy was quite real, the ability of others to acknowledge that pain was discussed as being part of a healing process. In the midst of losing parishioners, losing pledging units, and with resignations from the vestry following the introduction of a controversial program serving gays within the community, Grant admitted how personally wounding it proved to be. Yet through the experience he learned that he could let himself be vulnerable.

> I learned to say to peers and to the community, "I'm not sure about this. I'm not one hundred percent right. But I'm bit and I'm getting hurt. I want you to know this is hurting me." And when those folks left . . . when they left, I was able to say from the pulpit, and more importantly from vulnerability, speaking to the vestry, "I feel a personal hurt. I am spiritually bleeding over this."

Beyond admitting that the process of negotiating their way through an emotional conflict was painful was the recognition that it was necessary to seek support in order to be able to negotiate effectively. Of his support group comprised of other priests, Harry offered, "That's the most helpful thing there is—sharing with a colleague's group." Many sought emotional encouragement from other priests. Petra returned to school to pursue a doctorate, in part for the collegiality. She emphasized the importance of relying on fellow clergy.

> It's so essential to have other people who are in ordained leadership who you love and trust and who love and trust you. That you can just put it all out there and say, "This is the idea. This is where I want to get, but right now today let me vent." And to be able to do that is really important because otherwise . . . you take so much in that it can become spiritually cancerous to you.

Being in relationship with fellow clergy, even those with whom one disagrees, was of enormous value for Kelly. Moderately conservative and not in full support of gay marriage, she still valued the presence of the gay priest who was part of the group she attends regularly. In fact, she was very disappointed when that priest left the group. Kelly said she had appreciated the multiple perspectives and the longevity of their fellowship. She said:

> Even though we have all these different opinions, the group met once a week. We read the lesson for the coming Sunday in the context of the Morning Prayer. We've a pretty, for Episcopalians, a pretty long prayer time in the Morning Prayer. Then after Morning Prayer is finished, we talk about the lessons. That feeds me. . . . The relationships with that group are like thirteen years.

Both male and female priests alike reported that emotional support was necessary for their survival. Loretta reported that within her former diocese in the South during the mid-1990s she found, "The women tended to have their own support network. So the guys were often envious." Yet women were not alone in their efforts to carve out forms of support. Some groups included men and women; others were for women exclusively and some included only men. Regardless of the gender distribution, the support being offered prevented clergy from feeling isolated. Grant said that he never felt alone, even as he negotiated the most difficult conflicts during the most trying times. Over the course of twelve years he was part of a group that

> met once a month for three hours and we talked through all sorts of stuff: personal stuff, diocese stuff, parochial and liturgical material. . . . So I had a group with whom I could be intimate and did. . . . I could express resentment and rage with this group and did not only on this issue, but on others. I could weep, which I did find it particularly hard to do. We're men. We're not trained to do that or actually expected to do that.

In addition to actively seeking emotional support, some forms of support simply found them. Grant recounted an experience during a particularly embattled period when he was attempting to resolve conflicts over the introduction of a comprehensive AIDS program. He reflected on an important realization made during this particularly difficult time. He said he never fully realized nor appreciated the support he had from members of the congregation until the conflict reached its peak. In recounting an experience with a Jamaican congregant, Grant recalled:

> After one vestry meeting just as an aside he walked by me and said: "In the Anglican Church in Jamaica we're taught to pray every day for our priests. And I pray every day for you." And do I need anything else? Not really. So I think that was something else I learned. The silver lining of the conflict was that the depth of support there was greater than I ever assumed. I didn't have to work so hard for that.

The consequences stemming from a lack of this kind of support were also discussed. More than one priest surmised that without support, clergy became isolated and that this isolation paved the way for mental health problems. As Grant, who effectively utilized a network of clergy for support as he resolved conflicts in his parish, stated, "My sense from my peers who have gone through this is that when they either become strident or isolated, they're doomed."

Loretta recounted an extreme and sordid case that occurred in her former diocese, located outside of the New York tri-state area. She had observed the downfall of an extremely homophobic bishop whom she later learned frequented local gay clubs with a young man known to prey on in-the-closet older men. His subsequent firing of two members of the office staff within the small diocese in order to give the young man a job eventually led to his demise. She said:

> He ended up basically taking early retirement because the alternative was ecclesiastical court. Because there were all of these diocesan funds which were missing. But like he was Mr. Homophobia. And you know that really fueled my belief that to say no to homosexuality is to drive it underground in ways that way too easily go sick. And that's not peculiar to homosexuality. It's peculiar to driving things underground.

Resisting isolation and staying connected to one's peers was viewed as a major form of support that helped clergy as they negotiated their way through especially difficult conflicts. As Kelly emphasized:

> I think it's very important for clergy not to be loners. I think you have to see other clergy on some kind of regular basis. Otherwise, I mean it's dangerous. I don't know if this has ever been studied, but I would be willing to bet that the male clergy that have gotten into trouble keeping their zippers up, that most of them have not been integrated with the other clergy in their area. That they've been loners.

Focus on Other Issues / Resist Being Consumed by the Conflict

Another learning experience, reported by half of the clergy as having nurtured them as they tried to resolve the conflict, was to focus on other issues beyond the conflict itself. So not only did clergy focus on a higher plane, they also focused on other worldly issues as well. Being consumed by the conflict was viewed as problematic and detrimental to their success. As Grant said, "The idea is not to drown in the conflict." This strategy of diversification proved to be useful for Connor as well. He said:

> I was not single issue oriented. So the gay and lesbian thing was one issue. We were [also] doing homeless shelter, day school, food pantry, broad-based community organizing. So that's the other thing I would say to a clergy person. Don't get focused on one issue. And they tried to do that to us. "Well you don't want to go there,

that's the 'gay church.'" But now people say, "Yeah, that's one of many things that they're doing."

Many priests spoke about how important it was that they resist being pigeonholed and that they not forget to address some of the broader based issues confronting the church today. Bickering over homosexuality was perceived by Connie and others as a distraction. She said:

> It's sad to me that we can't then come together on the things that we agree on. You know right now if all the churches that were fighting about homosexuality came together to help people in Haiti, we'd be fine.

There was the suggestion that conflict, particularly conflict over concerns that generated great emotions, like gay inclusion, had the potential to pull the Episcopal Church away from its larger, overall mission. This was certainly expressed by Kelly, a moderately conservative priest. It was also echoed at the other end of the spectrum by a priest who is gay and met with conservative African clergy. In a very real sense Fiona's response was akin to Bishop Schori's willingness to hold her mitre when she presided at a Eucharist at Southwark Cathedral in London. Fiona said that her conversation with the Archbishop of the Sudan was especially humbling and helped her contextualize issues surrounding the conflict.

> It's just a whole other thing in Africa. . . . I mean he's got bigger problems. . . . I think we have to enter the conversation with humility. He's living with famine and war and genocide. And the fact that our church's stand is making life harder. I'm not saying we should change our stand, but I just think we need to have some humility about how we're talking to him. You know?

Clergy found that the effort to resist being consumed by the conflict was actually a form of support, as such resistance allowed them to conserve their energies and focus on other matters of importance. In recounting her experience responding to ongoing e-mail attacks by several congregants opposed to the Episcopal Church's efforts to be expansive and include gays in all aspects of church life, Petra spoke of how debilitating it became. She said:

> I do think conflict has a way of, it's like a black hole and it can really suck in a lot of other things that are going on and you don't see those other things anymore

because they're sucked into the black hole of conflict. And it colors everything that you do. So again I think prayer, perspective, conversation, and all of those things are really, really important. Balance.

Accepting Religious Contradictions

Nearly a third of the clergy voiced both concern and resignation for the religious contradictions they encountered as they attempted to resolve conflicts over gay inclusion. Grant recalled:

> One of the issues in the experience with the AIDS Center was that the people whose piety, and I mean piety in the best sense of the word, not negatively, . . . they turned out to be some of the hardest people with which to deal. . . . The negative surprise was that the people who on the outside I had presumed to be the most faithful were actually the ones who were having the most difficulty.

For Kelly, the contradictions surfaced on an institutional level. While she did not condone the behavior of the clergy in Africa who threatened the lives of gay men and women, she did suggest that their actions needed to be viewed within an historical context. The messages that the Anglican Church had originally provided to those in sub-Saharan Africa were, in her view, contradictory and partially responsible for current conflicts. She said:

> We told them homosexuality was a sin. And now we've changed our minds and we don't understand why they haven't. I mean that is so wrong! To me that is like we don't have any understanding of them, their culture, how they got to this position. We just want to say, you're wrong! You're wrong! And we're just so much more sophisticated. Well?

While she expressed concern, she also expressed frustration and some resignation as she discussed other religious groups that, from her perspective, were much more consistent and effective. Kelly went on to say:

> I'm sick of all the politics. I just don't think that that's the Gospel. I really admire the Mennonites. They're very active . . . justice ministry, the poor. They do a lot about

the death penalty issue. That kind of thing. They do foreign aid . . . but they're quiet. They're Mennonites!

Seeking Spiritual Support

Though prayer was often linked to spiritual support, only about a
third of the clergy specifically referenced the Holy Spirit. Those who
did expressed a clear recognition that they needed such guidance. As
Connie said, "I believe the spirit of God is so actively moving and if we
don't stop to pray . . . we'll be moving ahead with our own agenda."

While the overarching attitude was one of outreach—to conflict
disputants, the larger community, to clergy themselves, as well as to the
Holy Spirit—very specific attitudes made these forms of outreach possible. It is useful to take a closer look at these attitudes as they provided
the cornerstone of clerical approaches to conflict resolutions.

Attitudes

In addition to giving support to others and seeking support for
themselves, clergy cultivated an attitude that helped to set the right
tone. They internalized qualities that created an atmosphere in which
relationships were more likely to remain intact after the conflict was
resolved or reconciliation was reached. Not only did attitudes of compassion, trust, inclusiveness, and a willingness to let go of a need to be
proven right help to move negotiations forward successfully, such attitudes also helped clergy maintain personal equilibrium. For many the
issue of gay inclusion was less personal and much more of a larger social
justice issue.

As Osmond emphasized, the appropriate posture of a priest is quite
distinct from that of a boxer. This sentiment was underscored by many
of the clergy I spoke with. It was a posture that was sometimes assumed
with reluctance, but it was adopted regardless of personal views or frustrations related to the actual conflict. This attitude had a dual purpose.
It served as both their armor and their moral compass as they entered
the conflict negotiations. The adoption of these attitudes, however,
need not be limited to members of the clergy or to Christians. It is part
of an effective negotiation strategy in circumstances where it is our aim

to maintain healthy and long-lasting relationships with those involved in the dispute.

While the notion of an unconditional, a self-sacrificing, or an *agape* form of love may at times seem hard to grasp, it was quite evident in the attitudes and actions of those interviewed. No one used the word *agape,* but they often spoke of compassion, an almost paternal inclusiveness, as well as a passion for justice and a deep appreciation for the importance of leading with the interests of others at the helm.

Compassion

The majority of clergy, particularly when in the midst of conflict, emphasized a recognition of the importance of compassion. With regard to conflicts relating to the acceptance of gays, Dennis spoke of love as a gift.

> I look at love as a gift from God. Yes sir. It's not for me to decide who is to be the recipient of that gift. And between two people of the same sex, who am I to say that there's not real love.

Others discussed compassion in even broader terms. Connie, who spent years overseas as a missionary, stressed the importance of compassion and admitted that she is still striving to extend the type of compassion she observed in others while in Africa. She said:

> In Liberia I was with people who had seen others kill their children. Yet they knew what the power of forgiveness is. . . .They know God in a deep way. I've got to learn from them.

The importance of extending compassion was expressed as a deep concern of those who raised it in their discussion of conflicts over gay rights. It was also very closely linked to a belief in a fundamental tenet of the church that there was, in fact, room at the table for all.

Inclusiveness

A great pastoral emphasis was placed on an attitude of inclusiveness by a majority. Those who discussed inclusion were unequivocal. As Harry said, "I think there is room in this church, in the Episcopal Church, for everyone." Those who discussed a need for inclusion repeatedly echoed similar sentiments. Grant viewed it as a basic tenet of the Episcopal

Church, saying, "We believe that there's a table around which there is room for everybody and enough food to go around."

For Connie the ultimate goal was that the church be readily identified as diverse. Though her church normally holds separate services, one in Spanish and one in English, she indicated that her favorite Sundays are those when they come together in one service and are joined by residents of a home for Down syndrome adults. She suggested that a mix on racial, economic, and other levels is most representative of what the church ideally should resemble—one body. Yet with this inclusiveness came conflict. As she said:

> And the body of Christ says some of you are going to want to cut off a hand. And that may be because it's gay, or it's got too much testosterone because it's too something. And Jesus just said no, you can't! Don't do that!

Connie underscored her belief in the need and importance of providing as much room at the table for as many people as she could possibly reach. She went on to say that she would much "rather be wrong and have risked being inclusive and erred there, than somehow thinking God needed me to protect God's holiness by excluding anyone."

This sentiment was repeated in reference to a general population beyond the Episcopal Church. From Loretta's perspective:

> We are all on a path of us being willing to see us as bigger and bigger and bigger and bigger. And that Jesus' ministry pointed toward that circle of us being pushed out until it includes everyone.

Similarly, Petra offered:

> I really feel the narrative arc of the Gospel is a narrative arc of inclusion. That you start with Adam and Eve and the circle gets wider and wider and wider. And the momentum of the Holy Scripture is to include more and more and more people.

Osmond shared an incident that he said helped to shape his understanding of the role of the church as it relates to gays and lesbians. He said:

> I remember one gay man came to my office. He wanted to join the parish, and you know as he was talking at one point I just said, "Welcome home." And he just started

crying . . . that taught me about the power of inclusion and embrace. That helped me to discern where's God here? Well God is when the prodigal comes home, doesn't feel like he's allowed in, and you go to ShopRite and get the biggest calf you can!

Advocate for Social Justice

More than half discussed conflicts over gay rights in terms of social justice, those who raised it were emphatic that the church should be actively engaged in social justice issues of this kind. A belief in social justice was closely tied to a conviction that inclusion was central to the teachings of the church. But not everyone felt the attitudes of social justice and inclusion were extended to all members of the Episcopal Church. Kelly described herself as more conservative than the majority in her diocese, which another priest described as slightly to the left of Che Guevara. Though certainly not ultraconservative, Kelly stated that her particular diocese "is incredibly impressed with itself about how inclusive they are."

She went on to express a sense of frustration because in her view the church made a concerted effort to accept some, but not their more conservative members and clergy, and this saddened her. She said that they fail to include their own conservative clergy. From her perspective there is room for others but not for them, and this poses a real problem. As she said, "We're going to work so hard at being inclusive that we're just going to alienate this group and that's too bad." Kelly went on to recount an experience at a meeting within her diocese. When a particular seminary was mentioned, laughter and a general air of dismissal was evident because, she believed, this seminary was known for its conservative views. "Now how does that make you feel if you went to Virginia Theological Seminary? And I did, but I was considered a liberal there."

While Kelly found social justice issues to be of great importance, they extended far beyond issues of sexuality. She was, for example, troubled by what she perceived as a misplaced emphasis by one clergy member who was desperately trying to send money to a church-based gay organization that she hoped might be operating in Uganda. Kelly went on to say that this priest

> made a big issue of, "Doesn't anybody know where, how we can send money to Integrity Uganda?" And I'm like . . .
> "Well, there can't be very many of them. They don't

have any job in the church unless they're underground."
What about girls who never get to go to school? What
about children who don't have a chance at education? I
mean that, if you're going to send money to Uganda! The
priest's children have malnutrition!

For this moderately conservative priest, a lack of education for girls
and the very literal threat of starvation were some of the social justice issues of greater importance than gay rights. From her perspective,
these pressing issues were being overlooked by this clergy member who
was frantically attempting to support a gay organization in Uganda. Yet
other priests viewed the church's concern for gay rights as residing at
the very center of social justice issues. As Ellen put it:

The social justice thing is, that's the question. This whole
notion of whether the church is or is not going to be
accepting of all people. You know, embracing people who
are homosexual as part of the parish. That's social justice.

Ellen, a white, middle-aged woman who grew up in the South
during the end of segregation, described what she lived through during
that time as "bothersome" and said these experiences left an "indelible
impression." She expressed a need to work for social justice on many
fronts and said that included full inclusion of gays within the church.

For more than half of the clergy, social justice took the form of support for outcast members of the community. For them, the struggle for
gay rights was on par with other social justice issues. Petra brought a
personal set of experiences that sensitized her to a variety of gay issues:
her father came out as a gay man while she was attending seminary.
Yet she said even without that experience, she saw the rights of gays in
a much wider context.

I do feel it's a justice issue. So I would definitely view
that as a Commission, to address that within my ministry
with that particular congregation. Just as I would if it was
a civil rights issue. Just as I would if it was an issue for
women. I view it in the same league as those issues.

Connor personalized gay rights issues within his urban ministry and
found this was an especially effective way to highlight the social justice aspects and penetrate barriers within the congregation. He tried
to reframe the issues in order to help those in opposition identify on a
human level. He said that on more than one occasion he has found that

if you have, let's say, some gay men and you go into a parish setting where you're trying to really open the lines of communication, and they're willing to stand up and say, "You've known me for the last ten years and by the way, I'm gay." We're not talking about an issue here. We're talking about human rights. We're talking about *me*. That has usually been quite a transformational moment in a congregation.

In his experience it proved to be quite powerful when the discussion moved from "the issues" to a relational encounter. Yet social justice issues were also reported as yielding other consequences. While the goal was to be inclusive and to reach a resolution, several priests suggested that anger was sometimes inevitable and equally necessary. As Connie said, "Sometimes Jesus picked up a whip. Sometimes there's a time for that." Similarly, in spite of their efforts to be inclusive and compassionate, sometimes efforts to provide social justice led to a natural parting of the ways.

There was an overwhelming sense that there were occasions when social justice had to take precedence over inclusion. A definitive line in the sand was drawn by one priest following the introduction of one of the early programs designed for an AIDS/HIV-positive population. Though the program had the support of the majority of congregants, there were those who were not supportive, but continued to attend worship services and take Communion. One of the most difficult experiences for Grant involved an encounter at the altar during Communion. With some discomfort he shared the story of a woman who, two months into the program, made a point of

wearing, and putting on in front of everybody, latex gloves. And by this point there were people living with AIDS who were attending mass with us. And, you know, the snap of latex is unmistakably recognizable. And when it was over, I called her up and I made the point that you can't come back here. You can't be here this way. And I don't think we're going to journey on together. And she said, "You're right. You're right."

So while social justice and inclusion were key driving forces for the majority of clergy as they sought to negotiate a resolution, there were occasions when inclusion of social justice initiatives overrode a call for inclusion of some members of the congregation.

Trusting and Relinquishing a Need to Be Right

Half of the individuals I spoke with viewed vulnerability and trust as being attitudes that were especially conducive to resolving conflicts. For at least one priest this was the most important learning experience. The vulnerability of the arms out, palms open approach was accompanied by a degree of faith. While there were many practical, concrete steps taken by members of the clergy to resolve the conflict, a willingness to expose personal vulnerability, and a recognition that they would survive such exposure, was also highlighted as an important component in the process of resolution.

Only three priests discussed having had extensive training beyond seminary to prepare them for the types of conflicts they encountered in their ministry. Two mentioned that their training as community organizers was invaluable. For them, the element of trust also surfaced as paramount. Even with his formal training, trust was crucial in preparing one priest for dealing with conflict. In the process of resolving disagreements over the adoption of HIV/AIDS programs, 20 percent of the pledging members walked away from the church following a congregation-wide decision-making process. Grant offered the following reflection:

> I think the first and most important thing I took away from that is that actually you can trust, in this case trust the Holy Spirit, but one can trust . . . not giving the tiller to somebody else, but reminding oneself, through peers, through introspection, through whatever, that one may have one's hand on the tiller but that isn't the whole boat. That isn't the whole crew. You're not the whole crew. You're just merely the navigator. That's the only job. And actually, if one tries to be all the crew members, the ship will flounder.

Grant brought his thirty-five years of ministry and the power of reflection as he made that observation. A general sentiment expressed by others was that the more experienced they were, the more they were able to trust and expose their vulnerabilities. For half of the individuals I spoke with, trust brought with it an ability to relinquish a need to be right and the adoption of an accepting attitude. It was almost as if once they were freed from a certain burden, this smoothed negotiations. Certainly the opposite experience was voiced. The inability to be accepting was viewed as an impediment to resolving conflicts. As Ellen said, "I think a lot of conflict resolution is that we don't take people where they are. That we take people where we think they *should* be."

Expecting Positive Outcomes

Four clergy specifically discussed conflicts in terms of the positive outcomes that they generated. This was seen as a byproduct of being in a denomination that encouraged intellectual engagement through human reasoning. When asked how she would advise junior clergy members, Petra stated that she would encourage them to keep a positive outcome in mind and focus on God's presence throughout the process.

> I would say remember that God is present, the Holy Spirit . . . and that this is not a curse. Nobody's smiting you with this. You should look at it as an opportunity for growth, for your own growth, for the growth of the community.

Deference to Community

Two clergy discussed not only a concern for the community but also a degree of deference as well. One emphasized the importance of being mindful of church structures and spoke of being careful not to alienate the congregation. In discussing her response to the Conflict Scenario (see page 6), where a same-sex couple's request to hold a ceremony split the congregation, Fiona indicated that if the vestry was not supportive she would probably

> ask the couple to have the ceremony off-site of the church. I would still do it, but I would let them know that I thought it was too difficult for some of the members, and because I didn't have the support of the vestry, ask if we could do it someplace else that was meaningful for them.

While Fiona still advocated for gay rights, she said she believed that people needed to be brought along gradually, and she would not go against sentiments within the congregation by holding a controversial commitment ceremony. This appeared to be less of a concession and more of an attitude borne out of respect. The difference was subtle but distinct. While the line separating attitudes from skills was sometimes blurred, attitudes can sometimes be harder to define or identify. Attitudes may be more reflective of who you are while skills are manifested in what you do. So in a sense skills may be easier to replicate, as they are more often reflected in specific or clearly identifiable behaviors. Regardless of how they felt at times, clergy made a concerted effort to refine and apply a very specific set of skills during conflict negotiations. These skills are discussed in chapter 3.

Questions to Ponder _____

1. In efforts to resolve previous conflicts, what were my personal priorities?

2. What have been the two most dominant and opposing forces I have needed to balance when resolving a particularly difficult conflict?

3. When I look at the individual attitudes clergy conveyed on occasions when they successfully negotiated conflicts (compassion, inclusiveness, promoting social justice, trusting/being open to vulnerability, relinquishing a need to be right, expecting positive outcomes, deference), are there any in particular I find especially challenging to adopt?

4. What personal strategies do I employ to maintain my own inner balance?

CHAPTER 3

How to Cross a Tightrope

Insights alone were not responsible for clergy success in negotiating conflicts. It was their willingness to develop and apply specific skills that moved them forward in the negotiation process. As they learned to listen with patience, to facilitate, to utilize creative approaches from a place of humility, they were able to move through negotiations with greater ease.

It is difficult to cross a tightrope with fists clenched and arms folded. Rather it is with open arms that one establishes the balance needed to reach the other side. Similarly, the clergy I interviewed discussed the importance of assuming the proper stance and setting the tone for successful negotiations. This was achieved as they facilitated dialogue by actively listening and maintaining their patience. Being creative and examining the conflict and the possible solutions from many different angles, while maintaining a sense of humility, contributed significantly as well. Though seemingly complex and involved, these activities allowed clergy to establish and maintain their equilibrium especially during very emotional or delicate negotiations.

Facilitating Dialogue / Listening Actively

Of the numerous skills exhibited, many emphasized the role of dialogue facilitator and more than half emphasized active listening. Combined, these were the most commonly cited as being vital to resolve the conflict. Clergy members worked hard to not only bring parties together, but to facilitate dialogue whereby individuals truly felt that their concerns, needs, fears, and joys were expressed and, most especially, heard. When asked what advice he would offer a young priest based on more than thirty-five years of ministry, and having successfully negotiated many conflicts including those dealing with gay rights, Osmond conceded to the sometimes inherent difficulty of being an active listener. He said that nonetheless it was important to make

> the effort to allow a person to vent their view even though you'd really want to kind of hold your nose . . . and to try and do it arms out, palms open, instead of fists clenched.

Most of the clergy I spoke with were cognizant of the importance of including the congregation in the decision-making process. The strategies they outlined to overcome the challenges were comprehensive and designed to engage both those in support of as well as those in opposition to the conflict issue. Communication skills were highlighted as being necessary in order to achieve that goal. In discussing conflicts within her parish over services being offered to gay members of the community, Ellen, a priest with an extensive marketing background, said:

> In a situation like this, it would take a lot of dialogue. And it would take dialogue from being urged from the vestry, which is representative of the populace of the parish. And it would take dialogue from the clergy working cooperatively from the vestry. What you would have to guard against is not having it such that the clergy said we have to do this. This has to come from within.

Skills facilitating open and inclusive lines of communication were repeatedly discussed by clergy as being essential in supporting the community and in leading it toward a successful outcome.

Patience

Half of those I interviewed reported that unwavering support for members of the community was demonstrated through patience. Carole emphasized the need for patience in dealing with homophobic family members. She found it helpful to simply and deliberately choose not to fight over controversial issues. The importance of patience was also underscored by Fiona who, albeit somewhat reluctantly, sent a letter to the parish after they had called her to serve as their rector. She felt it was important that she identify herself as a lesbian.

Fiona's interactions with a particular parishioner, who initially left the church following her arrival, evolved over time into a close personal friendship. The town in which she lives is quite conservative and not where one would expect to find an openly gay priest serving as rector. As Fiona laughingly said of her town, it was "not exactly the home of diversity. . . . The only gay parade is basically when I walk from my car to ShopRite. That's it! That's the parade." She also recounted the story of how the relationship developed with this older gentleman in her parish, who initially was clearly disturbed by her letter to the congregation. She said she felt it was important to let them know that she was gay prior to accepting the position, but it was patience that helped pave the way for transformation.

This story mirrors the approaches taken by others I spoke with. They began on neutral territory and were strategic in their outreach efforts. Fiona initially asked the gentleman to join the finance committee. He had retired from a career in the financial services industry and had a great deal of related experience. By asking him to join this committee, she found a point of common ground. She was also very patient. She gave the relationship time and focused on other aspects of her pastoral role. So, for example, when the gentleman's wife became ill, Fiona visited her in the hospital, and in spite of the initial awkwardness, Fiona continued reaching out pastorally. Subsequent to the death of the parishioner's wife, Fiona made herself openly available to him and continued to consistently reach out to him. One Christmas Eve she spontaneously invited him to a party, and to her surprise, he accepted the invitation. In speaking of this friendship, which developed over years, she said:

> And since then we have had a sort of running joke about his first date in sixty years. . . . So we now go on dates about once every two months. And it points out to me that sometimes conflict is resolved over very long, slow periods as you build up trust. But that feels like one of the most genuine friendships that I have in the church.

Not only did it take time and patience to build solid relationships, these qualities were also required if one was to become centered. As indicated by Osmond, whose words were the inspiration for the title of this book, one grows into this place of centeredness. Early on in his ministerial career, he managed a difficult conflict in his parish and admittedly learned from his mistakes. When asked how he would advise inexperienced priests today, he said he would urge them to stay calm. Regarding his own behavior, in retrospect he said:

> I think what I would change a lot back there would be my own level of expectations as to what can be accomplished. Because my frustration rose at times to fever pitch. I internalized totally, completely. You know, overworked, sleeplessness, depression, self-doubt. It was a dark time. If I could have been more mature in my outlook, I would have been more realistic in my expectations.

Osmond went on to say that he believed it takes a long time for people to want to be changed. His resilience, his ability to bring patience to the midst of the storm, grew the calmer he remained. It was from a peaceful place that he was able to assume the arms out, palms open stance, and by allowing himself to become vulnerable, he conveyed an openness that he believed made others feel they were truly being heard. This all, however, came with patience.

Assuming Multiple Perspectives

The ability to examine a conflict from multiple perspectives and to fully empathize with each perspective is one of the major contributing factors leading toward a successful conflict negotiation. Many of the strategies discussed by clergy reflected efforts to take on multiple perspectives, or to frame and reframe the issues in order to reach a resolution. Nearly a third of those I spoke with explicitly discussed this during the interview and talked directly about their attempts to paraphrase and restate experiences in order to help others better understand the issues at stake. In reframing the issues, Connor likened the church to Thanksgiving dinner. He said he would ask congregants to think about their extended families, and often somewhere in that family structure they admit they have at least one gay relative. He then asks if they are included at Thanksgiving dinner:

> And I say that's what we're doing here. We're having Thanksgiving dinner every Sunday. Am I telling these people that they're not welcome at God's table? Is that really what you want to say?

By helping them look at situations in a new way, clergy reported that a change in thinking began to erode old biases. In some cases it was reported that the experiences had been, as Connor said, "quite transformational."

Creativity / Taking a Multifaceted Approach

A quarter of the priests said that in order to resolve a conflict, they needed to apply their creative skills and take an especially multifaceted approach. Various forms of communication were utilized, including one-on-one meetings, guest speakers, coffee hour discussions, newsletters, Bible study, and other educational forums. Or as Osmond put it:

> I would want to . . . in a number of ways, go to the community to educate. That means . . . a shotgun approach—not one bullet but many pellets in different directions.

In response to the mock Conflict Scenario (see page 6) read to each of the clergy at the start of the interview, the only priest who did not mention approaching either the vestry or the congregation-at-large was one not in support of same-sex unions. She admitted to being "stuck" in her views. This was clearly an issue that she had wrestled with for many years and Kelly said that the Conflict Scenario would in fact be her worst nightmare.

> I would have to be very honest with you and say I would rather not officiate. I would hope that in my most best I would say, "Let's talk about this and make an appointment for another time. And I would hope that I would say [pause] you know guys or girls, whatever. I have a real issue with this situation. Because while I think that homosexuals should have all the rights of married couples, I'm not there yet to say that it's the same thing as a marriage.

Humility and Flexibility

Two priests were quite explicit in their discussion of the importance of humility in resolving conflicts relating to homosexuality. Fiona also spoke of the need to be flexible. In recounting an experience early on in her career, she indicated that with time she had learned to lead while also being appropriately humble and flexible. She recalled a conflict with her senior warden over the scheduling of church school. The warden would become intoxicated and call her late at night and talk to her in a particularly abusive way. Fiona admitted that as she was new to the role of rector, her response was naïve and pompous. She reported that her intransigence stemmed from the fact that she

> was still sort of play-acting what I thought a rector acted like. And as a result I had a knee-jerk reaction and . . . a very rigid answer.

In retrospect she admitted that in dealing with that conflict and others, a certain degree of flexibility would have served her well. Had she been more humble, she might have been able to hear the underlying needs more clearly.

> And so years later I feel like I should call and apologize to her . . . ironically, because what she had was a good idea and I couldn't hear her.

So inflexibility and a lack of humility impeded the path to a viable resolution.

Beyond the acquisition and application of specific skills, a full range of additional components helped to facilitate resolutions. Personal and religious factors had an effect on one's ability to resolve conflicts concerning gay rights. The development of relationships with gay men and women, a utilization of spiritual resources, and views concerning the nature and history of conflicts within the church were the additional factors that clergy said had an effect on them as they negotiated resolutions. Of these additional factors, one of the most striking involved relationships members of the clergy had with gays. Proximity and the development of such a relationship over time played a role in clergy members' ability to negotiate the conflict.

Close Relationships

The majority said that they had developed personal relationships with gays over the course of their personal and/or professional lives. These experiences had significant bearing on their ability to resolve conflicts relating to gay rights. The perspective of more than one priest was altered significantly during seminary. Connie, for example, developed relationships with gay men and women and learned that what they shared as fellow seminarians was of greater significance than the things that separated them. As she discovered:

You find out it's always about relationship. It's always about finding out we have something in common. We have more in common than we have differences. You know that people's genital life is so little a part of what their whole life is.

While I did not ask anyone directly if they had close gay relationships, over the course of the interviews the majority revealed that they did in fact have such relationships. Fiona identified as gay. While out to her congregation and the church, she stated that she has resisted the label of "gay priest." She was also unwilling to take up the issue of gay rights to the detriment of other issues of greater concern. As she stated, "I really don't think that my sexuality should be important." For her it was not an aspect of her identity that she felt needed to be highlighted. She went on to say:

It's not that I want to hide it. It's just that . . . I think that that's about the thirty-seventh most interesting thing about me. So I'd rather you know that I play online poker because that actually tells you more about me than you know.

While she admitted that it has been an emotional roller coaster ride watching the church evolve in its thinking in relation to the ordination of gay clergy, her views concerning gay rights were surprisingly much more tempered than those expressed by many straight clergy. Clergy who mentioned having close gay friends were often unequivocal in their support. As Harry put it:

Many of my gay and lesbian friends have their stuff together more than other people because of the struggles they've had to go through and pressures they've had to work through.

Relationships with gays served to widen the perspective of clergy. One priest recounted a very sobering experience during the early years of the AIDS epidemic. He had taken Communion to a young man in the hospital. As is customary in the Episcopal Church for the priest, Grant consumed the remaining wine in the communal cup. The man then revealed that he had AIDS.

I was just absolutely convinced I was going to die. I had two little kids living at home. I went into the men's room at the hospital and was literally sweating and on the way out I remember figuring out how I was going to sit down and tell my family that I was doomed and of course I didn't know. I just didn't know.

Grant later learned from his physician that his concerns were unwarranted and that given the vulnerable immune system of the man with AIDS, there was a greater possibility that Grant was more dangerous to the young man than vice versa. Yet the experience sensitized him to the very real life and death issues confronting some gay men at the time. A different type of awareness emerged for Loretta. She grew up in a very liberal environment and had many gay friends in the United States. She, however, encountered a very different environment in England.

> Growing up in Berkeley I've known homosexual people all my life. It was never an issue. So when I came to the Church of England, I was predisposed to the gay guys because I'd always had friends who were gay. And what I found is that there were indeed a lot of gay people among the people in the ordination process with me, and then in seminary, and they were very misogynistic. This was just so different than what I'd ever encountered before.

While surprised and disturbed by the antiwomen sentiments, she did not turn against gays. In fact, these experiences convinced her that it was all the more important to acknowledge and bless monogamous same-sex relationships. From her perspective it was the failure to acknowledge the importance of that blessing that led to an "anything goes" and unhealthy mentality that ultimately threatened the well-being of the community. Loretta felt "very strongly that when it comes to the health of the family unit, raising healthy children, it doesn't have to do with the gender of the child's parents."

For her it was more the issue of monogamy. This was the sentiment of additional clergy. Several had gay relatives involved in long-term, committed relationships. As a mother, Greta described the long, slow process of acceptance that culminated in her agreeing to officiate at her daughter's commitment ceremony. She indicated that the journey involved a very gradual opening of her heart.

> Over the years we've had a number of gay people on the staff. It was almost as if God was seeing to it. "Look you're going to meet these people and you're going to understand that they're fully human beings. And as such

are made in the image of God and they have full rights as you do." So my attitude had been kind of softening. It was a gradual attrition of my opposition to homosexuality . . . because of my exposure to homosexual people.

Two priests in particular felt that a need for self-disclosure was in order. During their interviews they each came forward to identify their connection to a gay man or a lesbian. As Petra revealed:

My own feelings about this are very personal as my father is gay and partnered, not married, but partnered. So I always have to remember that that's part of what I bring to the table in this conversation. I mean even if that weren't the case, I believe, I hope that I would still consider this a justice issue. But when it really gets down and dirty as it sometimes does it's hard to not say, "Hey, that's my father you're talking about."

For Osmond, the support of a lesbian sister was as much grounded in Scripture as it was in familial ties. At the onset of the interview he paused and confessed:

My sister has lived with her partner in Washington for over twenty years and their son, my nephew, is terrific. And I could become like a pit bull in my support. But you can't do that pastorally. So I know where I stand. But I'm convinced I stand there because the prophets, the Scriptures, the New Testament have said, the clearest manifestation of depth in prayer is compassion. Anything moving in that direction tells me I am interpreting Scripture properly.

Osmond also recounted the genesis of a personal transformation process that began in seminary. During his first week, an assignment was given to read a book and discuss it with fellow seminarians. In the process of completing this assignment, he met a couple of students whom he described as "just really friendly" and they forged a fast friendship. While socially they were together all the time, he was completely clueless regarding their sexual orientation:

Until one of them came to me one night tearful and told me that they were breaking up. And I'm trying to hide my personal reaction as like . . . you're breaking up, I didn't know that you had . . . like broken in.

Osmond laughed as he recalled this experience. He went on to talk about just how naive he was.

> At that point I was so incredibly ignorant about homosexuality that I was kind of stunned. But as I'm listening I'm realizing this sounds like a heterosexual couple breaking up.

From that experience he reported two discoveries. First, though homosexuality was foreign to him, the feelings described by his gay friend resonated on a human level that overshadowed other differences. Osmond said that another realization made him more empathetic in later years to those who were homophobic:

> I remember thinking now this is actually helpful. If I'm experiencing this, open-minded, good-hearted guy that I am . . . if I'm feeling this, now I understand why other people are having a hard time.

Other priests I interviewed also spoke of relationships with gays and lesbians in terms of transformation and evolution. These moments occurred in the context of church or extended church settings. In one instance the transformational moment was spurred not by a gay man or a lesbian, but by a straight woman who was moved to support a cause that assisted gay persons and others with AIDS. As Grant's congregation struggled over whether or not to initiate this comprehensive program, he concluded:

> In the end I had this woman on the vestry who had spina bifida, sitting in a wheelchair, was on welfare, and she was power chair bound, and in her pledge of fifty cents a week, it was a sacrifice for her and it was the best pledge we ever got. And she was the one who on the vestry said this is something we have got to do. She was the prism. She was the Christ figure out there and I don't think I'll ever forget her.

Another priest discussed how he had seen self-identification change the dynamics significantly and positively when gay parishioners who had been closeted from fellow parishioners revealed their sexual orientation. Once a face was applied to what had previously been "an issue," Connor found that perspectives began to shift. This inclination toward receptivity following the development of a close relationship with gays has been documented in other research.

Clergy appeared to be more willing to bridge the differences that surfaced during the conflict when they had some type of positive relationship with gays or lesbians, but a willingness to be open factored in as well. A general receptivity in turn contributed to the resolution of conflicts relating to gay inclusion. For Dean, the comments of his college theatre professor resonated many years later and helped him in his efforts to be more receptive to the unknown:

> I had a teacher in college who said to us . . . actually he was a drama teacher and we were kind of rough and ready Texans who didn't care for drama. And he said, "Look, you don't know what you like. You like what you know. And you think these plays that I'm having you read don't speak to you, but just open your heart, open your mind, and listen to what the writers are trying to say." So I've kind of kept that "You like what you know" in my mind.

The willingness not only to bridge differences, but also to step into the unknown was especially evident among those with close relationships to a gay man or woman. The most successful negotiators were the ones able to bridge differences. Osmond's experience with his two friends in seminary was perhaps most emblematic of a particular type of empathy. His experience enabled him to create not one, but two bridges. He learned to identify with his new gay friends, but he also began to understand the discomfort felt when one was exposed to the unfamiliar. Thus he could begin to understand some of the roots of homophobia. Understanding the importance of this ability to translate the experience from the perspective of someone else, to genuinely understand the feelings of both sides, was for me a key learning point.

Prayer

Prayer was one of the additional factors that was spoken of as having influenced half of the clergy as they resolved conflicts relating to homosexuality. Those who discussed it as a factor raised the need for prayer with great conviction. Prayer also assumed many faces. It was placed in the context of being a guiding force, a personal nurturer, and a sustainer of others. It was a central force. As Grant said:

> I have a very disciplined and active prayer life. I am not reticent to go to the Holy Cross Monastery and spend an overnight there, completely detached from the rest of the world and I have a prayer bench and I pray (the best I

can). And I think a lot of it has to do with that. The idea is not to drown in the conflict.

Others were more emphatic. Connie, a former Evangelical, said quite simply, "I would pray like crazy!" In advising other priests dealing with conflict issues, she went on to say of prayer:

> It's the most important. It's the foundational most important. You've got to be listening to let the Spirit guide and speak. Otherwise all your good ideas are just your good ideas. But I do believe in prayer. I believe the Spirit of God is so actively moving and if we don't stop to pray, to be still, we'll be moving ahead with our own agenda and God may be moving on a different track.

Others encouraged their congregations to pray about the conflict issue. Harry said he would "encourage them and hope that they would continue to think and pray about it." Osmond on the other hand, spoke of a theological process "to discern what God wants us to do."

The distinctive role of a priest, along with prayer, sustained others like Kelly:

> Ok, so how do I get fed? I think prayer. I think being a priest. Sometimes you get, you know, when you go to the nursing home to see this person and he's a WWII purple heart and he's ninety-four and he's sobbing. And he's about as big as you were when you were ten. You know it breaks your heart, but it feeds you too. That you were able to be there and pat him on the back and acknowledge his misery.

In the end, as Connor observed, it becomes a very personal, individualized experience.

> As long as you can go home at night and have your prayer life and say is this really what you're calling me to do and you get the answer, "Yeah, this is really what I'm calling you to do."

Accepting Conflict in the Church

While few look forward to conflict encounters, half of the clergy I interviewed spoke of it as an inevitable feature of human life. Many were not alarmed by current conflicts within the Episcopal Church concerning same-sex marriage and the ordination of gay clergy. They viewed them within a much more expansive context. Many were able to embrace ambiguity, and several spoke of the historical ambiguities within the church. As Grant said:

> Well, first of all, Christianity by and large is a movement. It's a movement of reformed Judaism whose Messiah came and will come again as opposed to one whose Messiah is yet to come. So as a movement we're always going to be going through this. This is not unusual.

Though contextualized historically and viewed as inevitable, conflicts were still seen as distractions. Yet it was not enough of a distraction to deter someone like Carole from focusing on other issues of concern:

> Humans are going to have conflicts. It's part of our reasoning nature. It just is. And you know what, there are so many other things we need to be concerned about. You know, there are starving people. There are people without homes. There are so many things in this world that are much more important than the institutional church. I am proud to an Episcopalian. But that's not my driving force.

Though conflict was seen as inevitable, and while some frustration was expressed over the lack of media attention given to those positive outcomes that have emerged following conflicts within the church, an appreciation was also expressed for a process that brought about learning and growth. As Petra said:

> Churches have gone through conflicts like this and have emerged in a healthy place. No, it doesn't sell papers or whatever. But yeah, there are people who are really I think looking to the spiritual bottom line, looking to: What would Jesus have us do in this situation? What is the Gospel imperative here? How can we move forward with our own authenticity but living it out in this community that we love so deeply? And there are churches that have been successful in it, I know.

While some were clearly saddened by a potential split from the Anglican Communion, there was also a clear sense that they would carry on with the business of ministering to those they were called to minister to regardless of national or international church issues.

Interpretation of Scripture

For just under half of those I spoke with, Scripture emerged as a religious factor that affected their ability to resolve conflicts that related to gay rights. Connie came from a Methodist and subsequently an Evangelical tradition. Her evolution, and shift from a conservative to an unwaveringly inclusive stance, was gradual and involved scriptural interpretations as well as the establishment of new relationships with gays in seminary. Connie said that during that time, her perspective had shifted dramatically:

> Well, seminary, I think was huge. Scripture. I mean studying Scripture. I believe my change comes from my understanding of Scripture. And it comes in relation to that I got to know gay and lesbian people who were, who loved God, who were as faithful in their sense of call as I felt I was. So who makes the judgment? You know, it's kind of like that whole thing with Acts of the Spirit coming on the Gentiles. Well, if the Holy Spirit is at work in the lesbian or gay person, who am I to say [laughter] "Get out!" I can't!

Self-Confidence

Only three of the individuals spoke directly of the self-confidence they gained by going through a number of conflict experiences. Confidence emerged for Fiona as she increasingly relied on faith. She said it was important in spite of the difficult nature of the problem "to have the confidence to sit with it and to trust that God is at work in it in a way that I don't understand."

Congregational Responsiveness

Only two priests discussed the conflict resolution as being part of something they were called to do and Grant mentioned it with some reticence.

> We decided . . . together that this is something that we
> were called to do. Now Christians get funny . . . we just
> get weird when they say what they're "called" to do.

Sensitivity to congregational responsiveness, the interpretation of Scripture along with views on the nature of conflict with the Episcopal Church and Christianity as a whole emerged as factors to be considered. These also helped clergy personally manage some of the challenges that arose as they negotiated a resolution to conflicts.

Questions to Ponder _____

1. In looking back at conflicts I have failed to resolve, what do I now imagine were the greatest fears of those on the other side of the negotiation table?

2. If allowed to revisit a conflict I did not resolve successfully, how might my language have reflected a more humble, patient, and flexible approach?

3. In which ways can I reach out to befriend those whom I am in conflict with?

4. How do I acknowledge yet not become consumed by the many challenges that surface in conflict negotiations?

Part 3 | The Challenges They Faced

I

N AN ENVIRONMENT replete with distractions, clergy resolved conflicts by assuming the posture of a priest and by looking beyond the numerous obstacles in their path. They were required to negotiate a variety of conflicts while living under the weight of the Episcopal Church's complex history. For those most successful, it was important that they not be overwhelmed and sidetracked by the many problems that surfaced as they carried this weight. While they were forced to acknowledge them, the challenges were not their primary focus.

In addition to historical forces, contemporary divisions within the Anglican Communion and recent disputes among Episcopalians also surfaced as potential distractions. The impact of these institutional challenges was evident on both a psychological and a practical or managerial level. Some of the barriers they faced were part of the very foundations of the church. Yet the origins of Anglicanism and its embrace of the human capacity to reason in some ways also allowed for a philosophical response that offered freedom. Simply put, clergy did not expect everything to be perfect. Some ambiguity seemed to be accepted as a natural part of life.

Multiple challenges surface even for those of us managing conflicts outside of the complex arena of the church. Invariably it seems there are unique sets of competing interests vying for attention and seemingly designed to make conflict negotiations difficult. As demonstrated by clergy, one way to avoid being taken completely off course, is to simply acknowledge the presence of these challenges without fueling their power to distract. Episcopal clergy seemed quite comfortable accepting such ambiguity. It was almost as if by accepting the presence of ambiguity they diminished the power of the many components that were designed to distract them and thus minimized their fears. This is especially worth emulating when in the midst of complex negotiations. Clergy acknowledged all of the challenges confronting them, but they did not fixate on them.

If we feel overwhelmed when called to negotiate a conflict, it is useful to not only accept ambiguity but to dodge distractions. Clergy focused on their long-term goals and locked onto that vision, in much the same way that one walking a tightrope focuses on a point in the distance in order to successfully make it to the other side. This also served to diminish their fears. In the case of clergy, the focus was on a much higher plane. By concentrating on that plane, they were able to look beyond each of the challenges that arose without becoming consumed by them. In order to fully appreciate their achievements, it is important to examine the challenges they faced in the broad and complex landscape that is the Episcopal Church.

CHAPTER 4

Carrying My Mitre

Moments of Reform

1517 Martin Luther nails demands for reform to front door of a Wittenberg church

1534 Anglican Reformation

1789 Episcopal Church of America established

1974 "Philly Eleven" irregularly ordained

1977 "Philly Eleven" ordinations regularized

1979 Adoption of new Book of Common Prayer

1988 Barbara Harris, first woman bishop elected

2003 V. Gene Robinson, first openly gay bishop elected

2006 Katharine Jefferts Schori, first woman primate elected to serve in Anglican Communion as the twenty-sixth Presiding Bishop of the Episcopal Church

2008 Church issues apology for role in slavery

2009 Bishop Shaw III of Massachusetts approves same-sex marriage in his diocese

2010 Mary Douglas Glasspool, first openly gay woman bishop elected

There has been no shortage of conflicts and controversies within the Episcopal Church. It has a long and complex lineage of protest. It grew out of Protestant reforms and gained independence during Revolutionary times. Today, over social issues, it has become a matter of whether to amplify the conflicts or to seek resolutions. The intermediary process of reconciliation is like a long, slow, and intricate dance with two steps forward and one step back.

The Mitre Controversy

In 2006, a woman was chosen for the first time to serve in the most elevated position within the Episcopal Church. When the Nevadan Bishop, the Most Rev. Dr. Katharine Jefferts Schori, was elected as the twenty-sixth Presiding Bishop at the 75th General Convention on June 18, 2006, and invested at Washington National Cathedral on November 4, 2006, the Episcopal Church took a major and especially visible step away from Anglican traditions. While the Presiding Bishop is considered the supreme head of the Episcopal Church's 2.4 million members in sixteen countries and across ten dioceses, her very presence highlights differences within the Communion.

A significant number within the Anglican Communion continue to find it difficult to accept her elevated role within the church while others find it impossible to do so. This was demonstrated quite publicly as recently as June 2010 when she prepared to preside at a Eucharist at Southwark Cathedral in London. The Presiding Bishop was ordered to forgo wearing her mitre, one of the most visible symbols of the office. Apparently the mere presence of a woman displaying this symbol of authority was too upsetting for some. The order came from Rowan Williams, the Archbishop of Canterbury. Rather than offend those still in opposition to her appointment, she carried it instead.

While she had a right to wear her mitre, she elected not to. It did not take away her authority over the millions of Episcopalians at home. With or without the donning of a mitre, she remained bishop. Yet the act demonstrated her willingness to balance potentially competing interests. So she did not allow her personal interests (a need to appear in full regalia) to overshadow a seemingly small conflict with much larger implications (given the lack of full acceptance of women by all within the Anglican Communion).

While Bishop Schori's response may have provoked as much discussion and disapproval as the Archbishop's order, the controversy does provoke thought. Are there circumstances under which we are willing to carry our mitre? Or are there times when our own self-interests get in the way and prevent us from resolving a conflict? Regardless of how we may respond to such controversy, the Episcopal Church has grown directly out of a lineage of protest and controversy.

A Political Lineage of Protest

Over the course of its relatively short existence, the Episcopal Church has been politically influential beyond what its numbers might suggest. It represents only a small segment of the Christian population. According to the Episcopal Church website, there are 2.4 million Episcopalians. Self-identification figures are even higher. According to results of the 2001 American Religious Identification Survey there were 3,451,000 adult Episcopalians of the 159,030,000 adult Christians in the United States.

Though comparatively small in numbers, prominent political ties predate the American Revolution. As it is also often noted, many of the first Episcopalians were from the upper socioeconomic stratum and over a quarter of American presidents, including George Washington, Thomas Jefferson, Franklin Delano Roosevelt, and George H. W. Bush have been Episcopalian. Power, politics, and sometimes violent struggles have all contributed to the evolution of the Episcopal Church.

It is important to remember that not only was the Episcopal Church founded within a Revolutionary context, but it also emerged from a lineage of protest dating back to the Protestant Reformation. Within the spectrum of Christianity, Roman Catholics may represent the largest denomination, but it is Protestants who represent the largest branch. As a part of this branch, the Episcopal Church is linked to this early protest movement via the Church of England. In 1517 Martin Luther called for reform. By 1534 a host of social and political concerns in addition to disagreements with the Roman Catholic Church over forms of worship led to the Anglican Reformation. This movement provided increased access to the Church through the adoption of an English language prayer book and by holding services in English as opposed to Latin.

The Church of England was the first denomination to establish permanent ties within the original American colonies. Yet even during this early colonial period, conflicts separated the various religious groups. Views concerning the appropriate balance between religion and politics, for example, had an impact on early efforts to govern. Eventually the mix of politics and religion in the colonies led to discord as the founding fathers struggled to find the right balance between church and state. At times the laws favored one religious group over another, and Jews and Catholics were not among the most favored groups. Rather it was the Protestants, and a select group of Protestants at that, whose concerns were advanced. During this period of colonial rule, the Anglicans were one of the most politically dominant denominations. Many supported the American Revolution and played a key role in developing the new nation. In fact, it is often noted that the majority of those signing the Declaration of Independence as well as many of the key American military leaders at that time were Anglicans.

Following the Revolutionary War, tensions between the settled Anglicans and the Church of England led to the emergence of the Episcopal Church as a separate entity. In 1789, the formal name— The Protestant Episcopal Church in the United States of America— was adopted. So the Episcopal Church was truly founded within a Revolutionary context. It should not be surprising when struggles continue to surface in a contemporary context.

A Complex Modern History
of Conflict within the Episcopal Church

Conflicts have continued since the Protestant Reformation and the American Revolution and they have served to erode relationships within the church. In more recent times, especially over the last forty years, three issues have garnered much attention. These include the ordination of women, gay rights, and revisions to the Book of Common Prayer. Two of these issues are social issues and reflect changes in thinking within the society at large. This shift in cultural acceptance of what was once shunned, along with changes in church policy, has also occurred in relation to other social issues over the years.

The Episcopal Church has been willing to "carry its mitre," so to speak, over some social issues in a very public fashion. So, for example, while the Anglican Church did not take an early position concerning the abolition of slavery, there was subsequent recognition of institutional failings concerning this issue and a formal apology was issued in October 2008. On this and other social issues, the Episcopal Church has become increasingly liberal or aligned with what supporters would deem progressive views. In fact, the Episcopal Church is seen by some as the most forward thinking of all mainline denominations. Shifts have not taken place without due process and efforts to include those in opposition to change. Yet attempts to progress have been painful; some more so than others.

Of the three most controversial issues that confronted the Episcopal Church, comparatively speaking, conflicts generated by the adoption of a new prayer book in 1979, and the ordination of women, were contentious, but less controversial, than efforts to more fully embrace gays within the church. While Bishop Schori is the first woman to serve as a Primate within the Anglican Communion, and while this has led to many internal and external tensions, it is not nearly as divisive an issue as the appointment of the church's first openly gay bishop, V. Gene Robinson, elected Bishop of the Episcopal Diocese of New Hampshire on June 7, 2003. Bishop Robinson plans to retire in 2013 when he turns sixty-five. His willingness to walk a path of openness and humility, metaphorically carrying his mitre along the way, has not come without a high price. As he said in his retirement announcement given at the annual convention of his diocese:

> Death threats, and the now worldwide controversy surrounding your election of me as bishop, have been a constant strain, not just on me, but on my beloved husband, Mark, and on Episcopalians in the state.

Viewed jointly, the ordination of an openly gay bishop and the ordination of a woman primate have served to push the limits for a number of conservative Episcopal parishes in the United States. So much so that they have attempted to sever historical ties to the Episcopal Church in order to realign with more conservative Anglican dioceses in either Africa or Latin America.

These struggles within local Episcopal Churches are emblematic of the conflicts that exist across the global Anglican community. What some perceive as a crisis within Christianity over conflicting biblical interpretations and the rights of gays has placed a special strain on relations throughout the Anglican Communion. This includes not only the Episcopal Church, but worldwide affiliates as well.

While the Episcopal Church has often been perceived as one of the most liberal members of the Anglican Communion, the most conservative members of the Communion are found in sub-Saharan Africa, where membership is steadily increasing. Their position on same-sex marriage and their view concerning the ordination of gay clergy are, not surprisingly, at opposite ends of the spectrum.

Yet the current configurations, alignments, reconfigurations, and attitudes in Africa that allow for proposals to execute gay people in

Uganda, for example, cannot be separated from a forceful British colonial rule. Anglicanism accompanied the domination and the conflict-ridden experiences of colonialism. The growth of the Anglican Church paralleled an aggressive colonial expansion. While the British government established political dominance, missionary Anglicans established churches. Subsequently, as colonial dominance faded, the missions became independent Anglican churches and provinces, albeit part of the Anglican Communion, which is overseen by the Church of England's Archbishop of Canterbury.

Meanwhile, in the United States, the Episcopal Church has continued to move in quite the opposite direction. In one notable five-month span, for example, significant gay rights were afforded. In November 2009, Bishop M. Thomas Shaw III of Massachusetts approved same-sex marriages in churches within his diocese. On March 18, 2010, the Episcopal Church confirmed the election of Bishop Mary Douglas Glasspool, who was consecrated on May 15, 2010. She serves as the first openly lesbian bishop in the Episcopal Church and within the Anglican Communion.

To complicate matters further, in the fall of 2009 the Vatican invited disaffected conservatives from the Anglican Communion to join the Catholic Church. Such realignments and conflicts—played out within an international arena—have been spiritually painful on a local level. They have been financially difficult as well. Some breakaway churches in the United States have attempted to retain control of church property and assets. In the northeastern Virginia diocese, for example, this conflict led to much publicized legal battles over church property, valued in the millions of dollars.

In response to some of these conflicts, the Anglican Communion has initiated efforts to take a long in-depth look at human sexuality as well as homosexuality. It has encouraged members of the church to "struggle together" and listen as they seek to discern God's ways. In the midst of this struggle, a number of churches in the United States with strong conservative beliefs have moved on and voted to secede from the Episcopal Church. They have realigned themselves with conservative provinces or have joined the new conservative Episcopal Church in the United States called the New Anglican Church in North America. This latter affiliation is especially controversial, as the Anglican Communion only recognizes one official national church per country.

To fully appreciate the weight placed on local clergy today, one must take into account not only current issues, but the complex interplay between history and current events that has shaped the environment in which Episcopal clergy must find ways to resolve conflicts.

The Root of Complexity within the Episcopal Church

Understanding how Episcopal clergy have learned to resolve conflicts over homosexuality may benefit others attempting to negotiate their way through similar conflicts. Yet there are certain aspects of the Episcopal Church and the Anglican Communion that provide additional challenges to resolving disputes within this denomination. These challenges, however, can be seen to reflect some of the inherent ambiguities of life that we must all face in one way or another.

An important thread linking Episcopalians to others within the Anglican Communion involves the elevated and formalized set of expectations for parishioners. The elected governing body of representatives from the parish—the vestry—fills an important role within the church. They support the ongoing mission of the parish and handle practical matters involving property and finances, for example.

Yet perhaps the most appealing and troublesome feature linking all Anglicans, including Episcopalians, is their confidence in the ability of parishioners to utilize their reasoning skills. This ultimately has some bearing on their ability to come to resolutions over conflicts. It can be argued that this acceptance of reason has actually led to conflict. Yet it has also paved the way for an acceptance of ambiguity and for changes within the church. Rather than adopting authoritative interpretations without question, an increased level of responsibility is placed on each member to engage in a faith journey that embraces both the intellect and the spirit. There is the belief that all Christians should be in a direct relationship with the Word of God as reflected in the Bible. Reason based on intelligence and experience is seen as the vehicle leading to a better understanding of the Word. The biblical text along with teaching and traditions help Episcopalians apply religious understanding to their personal lives.

This mandate was in many respects revolutionary. Compared with the Catholic Church, it reflects a different way of thinking about one's relationship with God. Yet with this way of thinking also came responsibility—for the individual to establish his or her own understanding and for the church to in some way manage and care for those with differing understandings. This is no small task on either the individual or the institutional level. Parishioners embark on an active faith journey rife with tensions as individual understandings alone do not dictate church policies.

The church, and by extension the clergy, is expected to support parishioners, while at the same time clergy themselves proceed down their own path of spiritual formation and adhere to the dictates of their diocese and national church. Hence, all are challenged and not necessarily in full agreement. This ambiguity becomes part of a church life they must live with. Today because of these intellectual and theological foundations on which they were built, the Anglican Communion and the Episcopal Church face multiple challenges.

Placing significant responsibility on the individual to apply reason and to wrestle with theological issues creates a climate in which conflicting biblical interpretations can readily emerge. What must be done when the intellectual understandings of individual church members are in opposition to one another or to the church itself? Holding the community together as a cohesive unit becomes a major challenge, particularly when there are no formal guidelines for the resolution of conflicts. Forms of resistance may also emerge when beliefs based on reason lead to new forms of social action.

While today the call for same-sex marriage is one of the most divisive issues facing the churches across many denominations, the struggle for gay rights is only one of many sources of conflict within Christianity, the Anglican Communion, or the Episcopal Church. Opposing beliefs based on conflicting biblical interpretations have been a source of many conflicts throughout the years, with the Reformation representing just one notable example.

In a contemporary context, the ordination of the first female primate, along with the ordination of openly gay bishops, and an increased receptivity to same-sex marriages, has collectively placed the Episcopal Church in direct opposition to the views of a large and growing number of Anglicans. These ordinations may reflect the current sensibilities of many within the Episcopal Church and in society at large, but not all (Episcopalians or Anglicans) are in support of these decisions. So one is left with the question of whose form of reasoning is appropriate and should therefore govern behavior.

The Choice to Amplify
or Reconcile Conflict

While struggles within dioceses across the United States over efforts to fully embrace gays within the church have captured much attention and placed a strain on clergy and congregants alike, attempts are being made to narrow the breach. On an organizational level, the Episcopal Church has made some attempts to reconcile local beliefs with Anglican views and broaden understandings. Likewise, on the local parish level, individual members of the clergy have sought to balance their personal understandings with the emergent views of the Episcopal Church.

Those who disagree with current liberal Episcopal views have, not surprisingly, been challenged. More surprising, however, are the struggles of those whose understandings are generally in line with liberal church polity as they negotiate with more conservative members of their church. Clergy who personally endorse movements within the church to elect gay and lesbian bishops and support same-sex unions have at times struggled to temper their actions in order to reconcile related conflicts with peers, family members, or members of their congregations. Others have experienced a personal evolutionary process and closed the breach as their views changed over time.

It seems that now, as in the past with other issues that have generated great emotion, the choice is up to individual Christians to focus on what is of utmost importance. As the former three-term U.S. Republican senator and ordained Episcopal priest, John Danforth has pointed out, Christianity is supposed to be a ministry of reconciliation. Yet in the political realm, he notes that it has served as a particularly divisive force. Unfortunately, it is those who choose to focus on the negative divisions who receive the lion's share of attention.

The quiet ways in which clergy daily, dutifully, and successfully negotiate conflict go unnoticed. As the world focuses on conflicts concerning gay inclusion within church communities, some individuals have quietly looked to local clergy to help them navigate a difficult and unfamiliar terrain. The experiences of clergy presented here provide an alternative view of how disagreeing parties may work to hold a community together.

Two Steps Forward, One Step Back: The Process of Reconciliation

The foundational principles of Christianity include a variety of beliefs that coalesce in order to form a community where many members constitute one corporate body. Multiple and sometimes conflicting understandings within the Episcopal Church have led to breaches within the community, but they have also led to new understandings and opportunities for growth as well. While the conflicts are often highlighted, the long, slow process of discussion and deliberation that has taken place within the Anglican Communion has received comparatively little attention. For some time it has been engaged in a thoughtful, methodical, and prayerful process designed to help those within the Communion better understand human sexuality in general and more specifically homosexuality within the context of faithful Christian discipleship. A review of Lambeth Conference proceedings reflects the evolution of church responses to this and other social concerns.

Every ten years all bishops of the Anglican Communion gather to discuss issues of concern to the church at the Lambeth Conference. In recent decades they have considered and passed formal Resolutions concerning an increasing number of social issues. In 1968 they considered the ordination of women. In 1978 there were efforts to promote a social Gospel. Recognition of a need for further study on homosexuality was also put forth in 1978. Ten years later, Resolutions included the ordination or consecration of women to the episcopate and also in 1988 the first woman, Barbara Harris, was consecrated bishop in the Episcopal Diocese of Massachusetts.

In 1998, Resolution 1:10 was passed. This Resolution affirms an understanding of marriage between a man and a woman as it also acknowledges that there are those with a homosexual orientation. In addition, the Resolution calls for a process of mutual listening concerning human sexuality. In response to this call, the church outlined a formal Listening Process. It is worth noting that in formal approaches to conflict resolution, active and passive listening are tools used to improve communication in negotiations.

Through its own formal effort to *listen,* the Anglican Communion and the Episcopal Church have sought to encourage empathy and sensitivity while moving people away from deadlocked and divisive debates. Yet these efforts are not well publicized within a broader context. While creative ways in which to frame this Listening Process are outlined in *The Anglican Communion and Homosexuality*, it has not gained much media attention. Nevertheless, this book was designed to generate thought and help Anglicans become effective listeners of homosexuals and to develop a better understanding of their own as well as the opinions of others on this topic.

The most recent Lambeth Conference in 2008 did not produce a final Resolution resolving the debate over gay clergy or same-sex unions. Instead, Rowan Williams, the Archbishop of Canterbury, announced a moratorium on the consecration of gay bishops and blessings of same-sex couples. Yet the Episcopal Church has continued to move forward with the consecration of gay bishops. Not surprisingly, this decision further provoked a number of conservative Episcopalians and stands as yet another point of contention in a series of disagreements over matters of liturgy, gender, and sexuality.

With their actions, the Episcopal Church is poised in a challenging position—embracing change as it still holds on to deep and historical ties to the Anglican Communion. This process of evolution has been slow, painful at times, and nonlinear. So this is the thorny landscape through which local clergy must cross as they attempt to resolve conflicts. Faced with this medley of challenges, it was interesting to see how clergy resisted being consumed by them.

Questions to Ponder ———————————————

1. How might understanding current church conflicts within a historical context ease my burdens while trying to resolve disputes?

2. In resolving a conflict, can I identify a pivotal moment when I made a choice to either amplify or reconcile the dispute?

3. In what way have I visibly demonstrated my willingness to compromise? Or on which occasions have I been willing to "carry my mitre"?

4. How have current national and international church struggles affected me as I have attempted to resolve disputes concerning gay inclusion?

※ CHAPTER 5 ※

Resisting Challenges
Designed to Distract

The majority of clergy found it a challenge to balance the dichotomy between their pastoral/institutional responses and their personal/emotional responses while resolving conflicts. A suitable pastoral response required them to manage overarching organizational pressures without giving way to an uncensored response. They also needed to remain balanced while facing the potential loss of parishioners and financial support as they managed their sometimes-evolving views on homosexuality and gay rights. All this was generally done without the benefit of conflict resolution training. Yet as they focused on a higher plane, they managed to maintain a spiritual balance.

Values, moral responsibilities, and ethical principles cross secular and religious boundaries. The approaches derived from the experiences of clergy may help other individuals view their own conflicts as an opportunity to bring parties closer together. When we are able to focus our attention on universal connections and our common humanity, efforts to resolve our differences have added significance. Our methods may say far more about our personal and spiritual development than any loud confessions of faith might suggest.

It is important to keep in mind the fact that conflict can serve as an impetus for positive change. In fact, there would probably be much less diversity within Christianity, especially within the Protestant faith, had all Christians been in agreement. So when disagreements surface, the question becomes how best to move through them.

It is challenging to move through conflicts when historical issues and social differences serve as a wedge. Yet in spite of conflicts that span centuries, the Church has survived, and many would say flourished. Throughout these and assorted controversies, Episcopalians have been encouraged to apply their reasoning skills—a call that has sometimes served to exacerbate the conflicts. Yet how does all of this play out on the local parish level? How do priests manage their own daily expectations while living in the shadows of a long history of conflict?

The clergy who shared their experiences had been challenged to manage many expectations and avoid being consumed by them. This was not a simple task. In designing a successful strategy, they were first required to fully assess the landscape and identify the minefields. Some were more visible than others, but the most significant challenge related to balance. Maintaining equilibrium challenged clergy on many levels.

Challenges to Reconciliation on the Local Level

Balance surfaced as a key factor enabling clergy to resolve conflicts. There was no shortage of issues to be balanced. In addition to the institutional challenges that are apparent and publicly debated, there are personal challenges that must also be considered. These inner struggles included a need to maintain a suitable psychological balance in order to be effective in their ministries. The expectations that laypersons have, and sometimes clergy have of themselves, can be high and occasionally unrealistic. There is, in a very real sense, a pressure to be perfect—an especially unrealistic expectation. A clerical awareness of the pressures and the human tendencies and expectations may actually make some clergy more inclined to seek out the support they need in order to maintain the appropriate mental balance required to be effective.

In addition to adhering to institutional protocols, and the need for clergy to maintain their own mental health, there is an overarching obligation as well. These men and women chose a profession with a set of clearly stated religious principles, which, in theory, supersede other bonds. While balancing institutional expectations and their own psychological concerns, they must also attend to spiritual matters and responsibilities. This becomes yet another factor that must be balanced against more worldly expectations. Yet efforts to resolve conflicts have greater implications when examined within a spiritual context. The way in which we handle the conflict becomes a reflection of where we are along our spiritual path. This applies to priest, deacon, nun, minister, and layperson alike.

So this meant that clergy negotiators were required to be balanced in yet another dimension as they approached the negotiation table. These were not, after all, labor union negotiations. A negotiation style driven by power, dominance, and leverage would not have been well suited to resolving an internal religious conflict. So it is not surprising that a degree of compassion was evident as clergy discussed their approaches to resolve conflicts.

In spite of any negative emotions, clergy described an openness that allowed them to reframe their perspectives and maintain their equilibrium. In fact, they demonstrated a willingness to almost love their way through the conflict. Their efforts resembled what some would describe as a compassionate witnessing that focuses on our common humanity. By maintaining a balanced approach, clergy were able to exhibit an especially empathetic negotiation style, with arms open wide. Yet they did not lose sight of their own values, goals, or needs during the conflict negotiations. Rather, a creative tension remained that caused them to balance their actions between personal and pastoral motivations.

The Personal vs. the Pastoral

Of all the challenges clergy faced within the context of conflict resolution, one of the largest obstacles involved maintaining a balance between their personal and their pastoral motivations. A large majority of clergy found it a challenge to balance the dichotomy between their pastoral/institutional responses and their personal/emotional responses while in the midst of conflict negotiations.

Maintaining the appropriate balance and setting priorities are inherent challenges clergy must reconcile on a daily basis. This includes not only congregational conflicts, but matters of a spiritual nature as well. From a professional perspective, a clerical ability to reconcile also has bearing on members of the congregation. It has been said that ministers should be evaluated on whether they have had influence in reconciling people to God through their ministrations in the church. So clergy are required to not only balance their own priorities, but also to help congregants balance their priorities as they develop a closer relationship with God.

Being balanced meant that clergy needed to juggle numerous and conflicting responsibilities. Adherence to institutional and religious obligations sometimes created psychological stress. Efforts to attend to their own needs had to be balanced against the needs of those who relied on them for support. Yet in the end, by approaching the conflict as an opportunity for growth, they learned to accommodate new perceptions and in turn helped others do so as well. So in spite of the many challenges, they managed to balance both the internal and external competing interests.

Institutionally Balanced

Striving to achieve balance is central to the Anglican way of life. Dating back to the latter part of the sixteenth century, following the split from the Roman Catholic Church and the establishment of the Church of England, *The Laws of Ecclesiastical Polity* was written by the influential Anglican priest Richard Hooker. The impact of this significant work was long lasting. In it he underscored the need for stability achieved through the application of three distinct measures: Scripture, tradition, and reason, which he likened to a three-legged stool.

Priests that I spoke with also referred to this metaphor, often noting that a three-legged stool allows for stable seating even on unleveled terrain. Balance is thus achieved through deliberate design and conscious efforts. As the surfaces change, or as social concerns in contemporary times shift, the adjustments can be made accordingly in order to achieve a new balance. As theological systems change, Episcopalians can rely on this philosophical approach to establish balance. They are encouraged to question, make adjustments, and achieve a new equilibrium. And yet while Episcopalians are given the freedom to reconcile oppositions, this freedom also serves as a challenge.

So it almost becomes an expectation that Episcopalians learn to work through differences of opinion as part of their spiritual journey. Certainly they are not strangers to conflict. Rather, they are encouraged to seek some form of reconciliation among the opposing forces of Scripture, tradition, and reason in spite of the difficulties inherent in the process.

Institutional Tensions

The nature of the church itself was described by a large majority of clergy as both a feature offered and a challenge that confronted them as members of the Episcopal Church. This served as a fundamental challenge beyond current conflicts over the ordination of gay bishops and same-sex marriage. On one hand, clergy are part of a very hierarchical tradition, but they are also part of an institution that encourages individuals to apply their God-given ability to challenge, and to reason intellectually. Reason involves more than the mere dissection of ideas. Within this religious context it requires prayer, reflection on the Scriptures and the incorporation of experience. The process is neither simple nor infallible.

Thus, reason is not to be determined quickly or in isolation. Given the fact that multiple perspectives are considered it is not a process without flaws. . While this call for the application of human reasoning was described as being personally appealing, it was also discussed in terms of a challenge and surfaced as another element to incorporate into a suitable pastoral response in negotiating conflicts.

Historically, Anglicans have been known for turning to human reason in the establishment of church authority. Yet this contributes to a climate in which conflicts and controversies can readily occur. As Loretta, a priest who spent many years in the Church of England as a deacon, commented, "If you look at the history of Anglicanism, there have always been outrageous controversies." Ellen, who embraces the intellectual nature of the Episcopal Church, went on to say how important the basic teachings of the Episcopal Church are to her and how foundational they are to her thinking. She stressed that it is important "to go back to the fundamentals of why we call ourselves Episcopalians, that we are urged to challenge reason." At the same time she discussed some of the difficulties that stemmed from this approach. In response to recent conflicts within the church concerning homosexuality, she said:

> We've not been at peace as a church. And we're still not where we need to be. And we may never be. Because we encourage ourselves as a body to think and to challenge. I have a problem with any kind of extremism. I don't advocate extremism. I don't want the priest down in South Africa hooking up with the priest in Virginia, hooking up with the priest in South Dakota who is creating some

sort of cartel to overthrow the Episcopal Church. That's extremism.

Yet the complexities inherent in the nature of the Episcopal Church held a distinct appeal in spite of the challenge to reconcile independent thinking with an adherence to hierarchical boundaries. Growing up in a very liberal household in Berkeley, California, Loretta described what she found to be most appealing:

> Basically this is not a literalist tradition. . . . I mean the Episcopal Church is basically a thinking church. The liturgy and the ritual was one of the very attractive things and the fact that you didn't check your brain at the door. You know, don't tell me what to think.

A genuine affinity for the Episcopal Church with its multifaceted approach to establishing authority was expressed, even as the difficulties this presented were acknowledged. And yet the contradictions that surfaced were also discussed in positive terms. Harry was quite direct in his assessment:

> I love the Episcopal Church because of the three-legged stool. Hooker's three-legged stool is the beauty of Anglicanism. We derive our authority from three equally valid points of looking at an issue: Scripture, tradition, and reason. And if you give one of those three too much emphasis, the stool is out of kilter. And it's messy and it's not real hard and fast with rules. But that's a great way to have a spirituality, a religion, and a community too.

All did not embrace the complexities generated by this approach. Kelly found that these inherent challenges were beginning to overshadow the positive features and mission of the church. As she was somewhat conservative in her views, she expressed continued frustration on a number of fronts and indicated, with some reluctance, that a continuation of her relationship with the church following her retirement was uncertain.

> What I really feel is that the conflicts have taken away people and money and mission and ministry. Not just this conflict. The Episcopal Church always has something going on. Women, the Prayer Book. . . . In 1928 when they got the '28 Prayer Book, did you know there

was a split off from the church then? They became the Reformed Episcopalians.

Peter had weathered a number of personal storms. He had first-hand experience concerning just how difficult it was when institutional tensions played out on the local level. He watched as the church he attended during his time at seminary imploded. It was subsequently deconsecrated following a series of conflicts that began when his partner volunteered to help a Boy Scout group. Yet Peter came to view these institutional tensions within a much wider social context. From his perspective:

> The Episcopal Church in the past, and especially with the ordination of women, we've always been involved on some kind of grand social scale. So we've never had time to recover from one cultural movement or cultural episode before we move into another area of cultural awareness. . . . I think to really understand conflict you really have to look at the culture.

One priest made the observation that her Catholic friends do not leave their church in spite of severe differences of opinion with Catholic leaders. She compared this with the culture of the Episcopal Church. She said devoted Catholics had a very deep "brand loyalty" even when they disagreed strongly with the Vatican and its policies. In her calm Berkeley manner, Loretta proceeded to tell me:

> I've got lots of Roman Catholic friends and I don't know any of them who think the Pope is not, you know, the anti-Christ. But it's like, "it's my church, it's my culture. The boys can do what they want. You know, we're doing our own thing. . . ." Yeah, and for them it is a culture. It is a way of life, an identity. . . . Episcopalians, when they get ticked off, they walk. They always have.

So the general climate in which the Episcopal Church operates, a climate that encourages its members to be challenged, provides a complex environment that clergy are required to negotiate even before being called to negotiate specific conflicts relating to any controversial efforts to include gays within the church. Yet clergy perceived these contrasting views as simultaneously problematic and appealing. In addition to this overarching tendency, clergy are bound by the rules of the national Episcopal Church and by their local diocese. So within this context they must also find the correct balance between the personal and the institutional should their individual beliefs be in opposition to the formal policies of the church.

Psychologically Balanced

The psychological screening of individuals seeking a career in ministry is required in most Christian and Jewish institutions. It was deemed necessary and important even before the number of allegations of sexual misconduct filed against Roman Catholic priests began to rise. Just as there are theological competencies that candidates are expected to bring to their ministry, a psychologically balanced perspective that indicates suitability for ministerial service is expected as well.

Traditionally the screening process within the Episcopal Church begins at the local level. The priest along with members of the parish forms a discernment committee that meets with the candidate. Only with committee approval did a candidate proceed to the next level within the diocese. So from the very start, candidates for ordination were grounded in their community. A psychological evaluation is also required prior to the candidate being deemed a postulant for Holy Orders. Authorization to receive formal seminary training is granted only after these reviews.

Today there are a variety of pathways through which men and women enter the process to become clergy. This process includes both practical and spiritual concerns. Though psychologists make an important contribution, they are not qualified to evaluate certain clerical attributes. They cannot, for example, determine whether or not someone has indeed received "a call" from God to become a priest. What they can do is make a comparative assessment to determine whether or not a candidate possesses the traits of clergy who have been successful.

In addition, psychological predilections and imbalances that would make one unsuitable to serve as a priest can and should be identified to help religious institutions screen out inappropriate candidates. Hence, as a candidate for the priesthood, bringing and maintaining the right psychological balance are important if one hopes to begin and sustain a career in ministry.

The men and women I spoke with displayed a clear recognition of the importance of maintaining an appropriate psychological equilibrium. Those who discussed the personal toll that conflicts take on clergy were also generally the same ones who discussed the importance of seeking emotional support. The language they used to discuss the toll was quite sobering and reflected a depth of personal experience. Descriptions of the actions they took to resolve the conflict indicated that congregants, friends, or family were a first priority. Yet clergy were also keenly aware of the psychological restoration that they themselves needed in order to maintain the right balance.

Emotional Tensions

Emotional responses emerged as another challenge clergy encountered in the midst of conflict. A large majority of clergy reported being challenged to balance their personal response to the conflict on an emotional level, with an appropriately pastoral response. Clergy reported being mindful that emotions could surface in a hurtful way and that they needed to be sensitive to the emotions of others. Dean, who had many years of personal and professional conflict resolution experience, offered similar advice to his daughter and her partner concerning her partner's parents' hostile response following their commitment ceremony:

> They said some very hurtful things. But what I said to my daughter and her partner was just keep the door open. Don't let in hurt, or anger, or anxiety, don't say or do things that will close doors. Because once the door is closed, it can be *very* hard to open.

This proved a wise approach. The parents eventually came to accept the couple and have since been generous in their support of them on many levels. Clergy also reported that they needed to be mindful of their own emotions. As Petra, whose father is gay, suggested, "Definitely the most challenging piece of it in any conflict is taking your own stuff and trying to separate it out." Concerning the Conflict Scenario (see page 6), which posited that a disgruntled and wealthy congregant might leave the church should a same-sex union take place, Connie said in a loud voice, "My temptation is to say, 'Go, take your money, and go.' But I wouldn't." While Osmond, who resolved a conflict dealing with church support for AIDS and HIV-positive members of the community, stated that his sister has a female partner of twenty years. He admitted that while he could easily become much like an attack dog in her defense, he fully recognized that he could not take such a stance from a pastoral perspective.

Clergy were very clear in their understanding of the need to separate personal hurt or other emotions from an official response. They certainly did not deny these negative feelings. Rather, they acknowledged them and managed to put them aside while they constructed an appropriate response that was generated from a place of unconditional love. Sometimes it was not so easy, but with time they became more skilled. Fiona admitted that early on in her career it was her own defensiveness that proved to be her greatest challenge:

> One of the things is that when you feel attacked, your natural action is to be defensive and to attack back. Or to just explain why that person's view has no merit . . . whatever. So for me one of the real tricks is to stay in that nonjudgmental and nondefensive place. And that's easier to say than it is to do.

When I asked another priest, Connie, what was the greatest challenge she faced in her conflict with family members concerning their views on homosexuality, she too admitted that balancing her emotional response with a more compassionate response was sometimes extremely difficult.

> I guess what's been the hardest is holding my tongue. Not wanting to just dismiss people. Because when you do begin to see things differently, it's very hard to not understand why people aren't in the same place that you are now.

As her own views on homosexuality evolved over more than a decade, she acknowledged that it would take time for the views of family members to change as well. While a balance between an emotional response and a suitable pastoral response was in order, the idealized pastoral response presented by clergy was not one of meekness. There was love, but it was not blind. It was not simply a matter of ignoring emotions, but of channeling them appropriately and purposefully. Paternal love is not without its critique of the beloved. In assessing the role of fellow priests, Connor, one of several priests with more than thirty years of ministerial service, suggested:

> Too many clergy feel like "well I can't be the agitator because then they won't love me. Or they're going to get angry with me." Well, they got angry with Jesus. If you're going to do this, you've got to push them. How many times do we as parents know that our kids get angry with us because of what we're trying to do? Anger is good. But

> I think a lot of clergy get very much afraid of anger and
> therefore try to avoid it at all costs.

Regardless of whether or not a particular moment in the conflict resolution process called for anger or for patience, one thread ran through the center of clergy responses. The interviewees indicated that they were careful to balance those emotions with a demonstrated concern for each parishioner or the other individuals involved in the conflict. Their focus was on a higher plane that emphasized inclusion and a nurturing of the entire community.

So while Connor believed that anger was appropriate at times, he went on to say that regardless of which side of the conflict parishioners supported, he made an extra effort to demonstrate that he was there for *all* of them in *all* of their pastoral needs. As love was emphasized, the conflict was diminished to a great extent and the bonds that held them together tightened. Others echoed these sentiments. Grant, another veteran priest with a great deal of experience in community organizing, said it was the individual personal relationships that he was most sensitive to. He strove to pay attention not only to his emotions, but also to the feelings of individual parishioners. So when operating from a position infused with love, as Grant suggested:

> One pays attention to the politics, not only the politics
> of the institution, but the personal politics. I was careful
> to make sure that particularly those people who were
> feeling angry and upset, and knew already what my posi-
> tion was, didn't feel that this conflict was going to have
> us alienated.

Clergy indicated that they were fully aware of their responsibilities and conscientious in their efforts to manage their own emotional responses in order to deal effectively with the emotions of others. Time and time again it was demonstrated by clergy that while they experienced a full range of emotions, their paramount concern was for the individual members of their communities.

This sensitivity to the needs of the community was really the linchpin for all clergy. It was perhaps best characterized in an urban parish that had experienced hardships and, at the time of the conflict, was on the verge of renewal. Connor utilized a strategy that helped parishioners begin to address their underlying emotional concerns and gain support from the community of worshipers. In an exercise called "Tell Me Your Hopes, Fears, Joys, and Sorrows," he had congregants take a sheet of paper and jot down their corresponding concerns for the congregation:

> And we'd just talk about it. We'd use it as a tool. And I guess the stuff you would call conflict would come up in fears or sorrows. "I'm afraid this is going to happen." But man, once you get somebody to put the fear out on the table, it's like all of a sudden. . . . Well it's like five of the people come up and say I'll hold your hand through that. I will be with you.

When the conditions shift as they did for the parishioners in Connor's parish and disputants are genuinely encircled in love, the dynamics are changed. As empathy rises, it becomes much easier to follow the path to reconciliation and resolution. Efforts to temper their own personal hostilities and nurture congregants were discussed by clergy as genuine concerns rather than as strategies for success.

In addition to their concern for others, there was also the understanding that the process of loving their way to a resolution could be personally costly for individual members of the clergy. According to Grant:

> People by and large want to do the right thing. The only parenthesis is that it does take a toll. It takes a toll of energy and attention and sometimes it hurts, it hurts.

A secondary challenge on the emotional level required clergy to seek out emotional support to address their own personal needs. Clergy were called to balance their efforts to care for others with a need to care for themselves. They recognized that they needed to receive nurturing just as they nurtured their congregants. They expressed a need to feed themselves on a personal level in order to be able to respond pastorally to feed and nurture others.

These tensions between a pastoral approach and personal inclinations surfaced on two levels—institutional and emotional. Although clergy valued the tenets of the Episcopal Church that encouraged the insertion of individual human reasoning in determining church authority, they also acknowledged that they were challenged by the very climate that they so valued. Clergy were required to manage their own emotions along with those of congregants in order to provide a suitable pastoral response. They tempered their personal emotions when appropriate and they also sought emotional support.

The path taken by clergy to resolve conflicts was very much akin to walking across a tightrope. They were surrounded by challenges, out in the open, and their actions were there for all to see. Yet they could not allow themselves to be distracted by these challenges. Establishing and maintaining the appropriate balance was of utmost importance. It was especially challenging because it was necessary to find equilibrium on both the institutional and the emotional levels. Yet other obstacles also emerged to distract clergy from their primary goals.

Additional Challenges

In addition to the challenge of maintaining a suitable equilibrium, clergy discussed other psychological and practical matters that had the potential to take them off course.

Beliefs concerning Homosexuality

More than half of clergy I spoke with admitted that their views and beliefs regarding homosexuality challenged them as they sought to resolve conflicts. For many clergy who supported same-sex unions, their beliefs affected the approach they took to resolve the conflict. While supporting the community as a whole was important, clerical views regarding homosexuality also guided their behavior. Harry, who supported full inclusion for gays within the church, indicated that if facing a conflict in the congregation over whether or not to perform a same-sex union ceremony, he would open the issue up to the entire congregation, encouraging discussions and bringing in guest speakers. He also said, "I would only bring in people who were pro with the gay issue."

Beliefs concerning homosexuality also surfaced in other ways. Loretta, who spent many years in the Church of England as a deacon, experienced multiple conflicts. She discovered that there were "a lot of gay people in the ordination process . . . and they were very misogynistic." The fact that a priest bit her hand rather than allow a woman to retain possession of the chalice during the Eucharist and other interactions of this kind, along with her observations of gay clergy led her to the following conclusion:

> The gay community exists among the clergy, always has and always will. When it is out in the open, the same standards of responsible monogamy are expected of all. When it is in the closet, you can do as you like. . . . It is harmful.

As a result of these experiences, she stated that it was important to openly embrace monogamous same-sex unions to bring couples in to receive full support of the community just as heterosexual couples were offered support from the church community. Based on her personal observations, it was her perception that bad behavior stemmed in part from a closeted existence. In her view, the more that was brought out into the open, the better for all concerned.

While Kelly shared the view that isolation led to difficulties and sometimes inappropriate behavior, she was a more conservative priest. She did not, for example, view same-sex unions as being on par with heterosexual marriage. She said that her beliefs would serve as an impediment and prevent her from moving forward in negotiations to hold a commitment ceremony at the church, as was discussed in the Conflict Scenario (see page 6). "I would tell them that I have struggled with this for years and I just don't quite see it as the same thing as a marriage." She would not bring the issue to the congregation or embark on an effort to educate the parish because her personal views would prevent her from officiating at a same-sex union. In the end she indicated that she would feel compelled to refer the couple to another priest who could support their needs.

Loss of Parishioners

The potential loss of parishioners was voiced as a concern for slightly more than half of the clergy, and it was discussed in terms akin to the loss of a family member. Grant recounted an episode that caused a significant number of parishioners to leave the parish. Of this he said, "I missed these people. It literally personally hurt me." Others echoed this sense of personal loss. In some circumstances clergy offered to find another church home for congregants. With some sadness and with a sense of resignation, Petra indicated that under certain circumstances a farewell was in order:

> To say you have the option to leave if after everything that we've done and said and talked about and compromised on, you still don't feel at peace, then that might be what you need to do for awhile. But that's a really hard thing to say. Even after eighteen years of ministry, it takes a lot of courage to be able to do that.

In her protracted conflict with two parishioners, Petra received regular and lengthy e-mails from them expressing their discontent with the Episcopal Church following the election of Gene Robinson as the Bishop of New Hampshire. They had left an Evangelical tradition to join the Episcopal Church, and they were deeply disturbed by the consecration of an openly gay bishop. Their e-mails, as she described them, were quite involved and more akin to legal documents. In retrospect, she said it would have been more productive had she and her senior rector pressed for more face-to-face dialogue instead of responding with line-by-line responses via e-mail. While the couple remained in the parish, Petra believed they were not so much interested in reaching a resolution as they were in voicing their ongoing critique of the Episcopal Church. She concluded:

> Sometimes you have to say good-bye to people. And I do believe there are people who are really looking for a reason to be resentful and to feel shut out. And I think at that point, I mean we turn ourselves inside out in the church not to alienate anybody and to keep everybody in the pew. And that's a good thing, but I think there's a limit to it.

The loss of parishioners was not a matter clergy took lightly even as they viewed it as inevitable under certain circumstances. Yet while it was raised as a very real concern, only one interviewee indicated that it altered her behavior. This was true for clergy even when there was a direct connection to a potential decrease in financial revenues.

Loss of Financial Support

Only three priests raised the issue of financial loss as a potential challenge. Like the potential loss of parishioners, however, it did not appear to alter the actions taken by clergy. In fact, it was noted that while parishes lost some members over conflicts relating to gay inclusion, their stance on a controversial issue also served to attract new members and thereby new financial pledges. The "profits and losses" were seen in much larger terms. As Grant said:

> I've been in a parish where 20 percent of the pledging units walked away. It was over the issue of HIV/AIDS. And they left. And in the end, of course, we recovered and then some. Because other folks came and said, "Oh, that's what this church is really about. It's not a club and prayer on Sunday. It is a place that cares about the world."

Lack of Conflict Resolution Training

While several clergy commented on their lack of training, Petra was the only one who discussed an overt feeling of being hampered by the lack of relevant preparation. In fact, she expressed a desire for specific formal conflict resolution training. She said that members of the clergy were especially in need of it:

> I think we should all have a lot more ongoing training in conflict resolution. I think it should be demanded. Because that's part of life. It's part of community life and it's especially true in the church because everyone brings their stuff to church.

While clergy faced many challenges in their attempts to resolve conflicts over some aspect of gay inclusion, the greatest challenge involved a clerical need to balance institutional, psychological, and religious expectations. They did not become consumed by the many challenges that surrounded them on all sides and at many different levels. Instead they responded to the challenges by maintaining their posture and keeping sight of their ultimate goals.

Finding and maintaining the correct balance was a key element leading to successful conflict resolutions. On the institutional level, clergy recognized a need to adhere to dictates of their denomination. Yet they managed to accommodate their own personal understandings. They also indicated that they attempted to balance their personal inclinations and needs with a response that addressed the needs of their community. Clergy expressed a strong desire and willingness to work toward reconciliation in spite of sometimes painful differences over gay inclusion. As they outlined the strategies they employed to resolve conflicts, they conveyed a sense of conviction. It was almost as if they were the chosen ambassadors charged with a responsibility to bring about reconciliation. This understanding helped pave the way to a resolution.

In spite of personal frustrations, the tone clergy attempted to convey during the conflict was very much in keeping with the idea that peace and understanding should accompany educational efforts to mend breaches within the community. Or that "the servant of the Lord must not strive; but be gentle unto all men, apt to teach, patient" (2 Tim. 2:24). This is not to suggest that clergy were lacking in strong opinions. On the contrary, their actions indicated that they made a conscious effort to appropriately channel their strong feelings for a greater good.

Questions to Ponder

1. What have been some of the major obstacles I have faced when trying to resolve conflicts?

2. In recalling a particular conflict I have tried to negotiate, what would I now do to visibly demonstrate my sensitivity to the needs of the disputants?

3. In which circumstances have I been effective in separating a personal response to a conflict from a less self-centered and more caring response?

4. What type of learning experiences have I found to be the most valuable?

Part 4 | How They Learned

OCIAL INTERACTIONS AND a continuum of experiences contributed to the learning process. Before they could move
forward, the process began in earnest as clergy adopted a
priestly attitude with arms out and palms open, as discussed
in section two. As they were able to remain centered and
focus on a higher plane, their ability to move along the path leading
to resolution improved. The challenges they overcame were historical,
complex, and numerous, as outlined in section three. Yet an appreciation for the larger context in which they were called to resolve conflicts enabled them to remain centered, balanced, and focused on their
priorities as they moved forward with success. This learning process
did not occur overnight. Rather it was part of an ongoing cycle of trial
and error.

In section four, the components of this learning cycle are examined. The general learning strategies utilized by clergy to meet the
assorted challenges they faced were tied to their social environment.
How they learned to do what they did is examined in chapter 6. As
clergy are often thrust into conflict situations without the benefit of
formal training, they are almost forced to rely upon their creativity and
faith. Their reliance on informal social interactions was in part borne
out of necessity. As they were forced to respond they had no choice
but to move past feelings of inadequacy and isolation. As they gained
experience resolving complex issues, their confidence grew slowly and

incrementally expanded with each subsequent conflict resolution they were called to resolve. This confidence increased only as they were willing to step into the cycle of learning.

In chapter 7 the learning strategies employed by clergy are more closely examined. Individuals often learn in relation to others. As the clergy I interviewed were also generally resolving conflicts within a community of Christians, the strategies they employed to resolve the conflict often took the unique nature of the community into account. Clergy were drawn to informal strategies that allowed for social learning. The effectiveness of their strategies is examined through a Christian, an adult learning, and a conflict negotiator's lens.

CHAPTER 6

Paving the Way for
Meaningful Social Interaction

It was important that clergy prepare themselves before they encountered the host of challenges that confronted them in their efforts to negotiate a resolution. They also needed to approach the learning process with a degree of receptivity. As they were able to shift their thoughts, and almost relax into the notion that repetition was a necessary part of the process, they began to learn how to resolve the conflict effectively. This entire process was hinged on faith. Their faith promoted confidence and they were then able to look to their respective communities for collaborative solutions that utilized past experiences.

How Clergy Learned to
Meet the Challenges

Conflicts were both created and resolved in the midst of social interactions. Yet it was a two-tiered process with the first preparing them for the next. Clergy needed to prepare themselves by assuming the arms out and palms open position before they could move forward effectively. Ideally, they began with introspection and then moved on to social engagement. Just as one is unable to solve an equation without first being introduced to a numeric system, clergy were unable to successfully resolve conflicts without first becoming mentally and spiritually prepared.

Preparation for Learning

Preparation involved creating a balanced mindset. For the majority of clergy I spoke with, maintaining balance while surrounded by a host of challenges required many internal preparations. Details pertaining to the strategies and skills they developed to prepare themselves are discussed in section two. In a broader sense, however, these preparations involved a shift in thinking as well as an acceptance of the need for repetition and the willingness to step out in faith. Clergy maintained equilibrium not through avoidance of conflict, but by turning themselves over to the process. This shift in perspective was possible once they focused on their faith instead of their fears. As one priest said, it is important to understand that one is not being smote.

By refusing to place themselves in the role of victim, and by adopting a mindset that saw the potential for good in the midst of conflict, they were prepared for whatever emerged. The conflicts could relate to simple matters or spiritual matters. Whether it was a dispute over the selection of a hymn, or inner conflicts pertaining to life and death issues, there was a cumulative benefit clergy received as they negotiated their way through an assortment of disputes. It was not simply the nature of the conflicts that they resolved but the process of negotiating a resolution that helped them to refine their skills. Each negotiation prepared them for the next. The experience of having negotiated any conflict in the past helped them to successfully negotiate highly charged conflicts like those relating to gay inclusion. So the most successful clergy were able to view all forms of conflict as learning opportunities.

Over the course of their ministries, successes and failures developed into a genuine reservoir of talents available for future use. Thus repetition was a key component of the learning process. Each time clergy were willing to venture out onto the tightrope leading them to a resolution they did so with greater confidence. This confidence was integrally linked to their ability to see the conflict within a wider context and fully believe that an invisible safety net was in place. Each time they crossed the tightrope and survived—even the missteps and occasional falls—they came to believe that safety measures were in place that would enable them to weather future accidents. Thus, with each subsequent attempt they could more readily maintain their balance and cover a greater distance along the path leading to a resolution.

As faith replaced fear, it became much easier to concentrate on the most productive collaborations. Once clergy were centered and focused on their goal, shouts from the crowd or other distractions were minimized. While human interactions were the greatest source of conflict, they also provided the greatest source of opportunities for support and growth. Even those who benefited from formal training learned from their interactions with others. They did so by watching and reaching out to peers, mentors, and role models. Parishioners in turn learned as they observed clergy and interacted with fellow parishioners. While supplemental "book learning" or learning in formal classroom settings was helpful, an informal seat-of-your-pants applied learning provided the most visceral and lasting experiences.

Social Learning and Collaborating with Others

Each of the men and women I interviewed had at some point learned to resolve conflicts through informal means. It was social and collaborative learning that emerged as the primary form of informal learning that led to the resolution of conflicts over gay inclusion. Collaborative efforts are consistent with the communal nature of Christianity. Being in relationship with others is a key component of this religious experience. Therefore it is not surprising that clergy often tried to be as inclusive as possible, incorporating a large number of individuals into the learning process.

Yet as several priests emphasized, collaboration was not to be confused with an abdication of responsibility. Barclay said he learned that while communication and collaboration were important, ultimately there were times when one simply had to take a stand, set certain parameters, and move forward. Initially in his parish, he said:

> We'd have lots of conversations. We need to break through this together, find out what the concerns are. But what I have learned is that when you do that . . . it's like the healthcare bill in Washington. You get these wild and really rabid emotional responses that aren't grounded in really any reality that I can understand. You have to sort of stop and say, "Now wait a minute. We just said something that we don't really say to each other as Christians." You have to say, "What are the rules here?"

While collaboration with others was deemed important, this need for maintaining civil discourse, in spite of the emotional nature of the conflict, was underscored by others. Several spoke of situations where parishioners needed to be reminded of appropriate boundaries when discussing conflict issues. Yet in spite of the inherent difficulties and risks involved in group efforts, inclusion remained paramount. This contributed to the balancing act clergy were engaged in. They attempted to be creative and inclusive while they also managed to discourage hurtful behavior.

Yet real collaborative learning encompasses much more than simply managing the discourse of individuals who happen to be in the same room. It involves the formation of new opinions generated by a genuine exchange of ideas. The strategies utilized by clergy were often designed to elicit dynamic input from group members. As one priest explained, the purpose was not to tell others how wrong they were. The goal was to struggle together and help one another figure out a shared solution.

In spite of the strain, the most fruitful negotiations were described as being more collegial than adversarial in tone. Even when their views differed significantly from those with whom they were negotiating, clergy reported that they tried to include as many concerned individuals as possible. With her passionate and Evangelical roots, Connie stressed the long-term value of incorporating input from a broad spectrum within the community. In discussing efforts to resolve conflicts between white and Latino congregants in her current parish, she said:

> I can make a decision, the vestry can make a decision, but if we don't take it to the whole parish and say what do you think. . . . What we need to do is to hear people. So far in my church, that has managed to diffuse so much because people have said: "I know you took a different decision, but thank you for hearing me."

The desire to be heard was an overarching sentiment. In discussing the Conflict Scenario read at the start of each interview (see page 6), nearly everyone I interviewed said that they would take the conflict to the congregation and engage them in the process of reaching a resolution. On any number of issues relating to efforts to more fully include gays within the church, Ellen said she simply returned to the precepts of the Episcopal Church. She stressed just how important it was to include the vestry, even for and perhaps especially when it came to such emotional issues. She also underscored the collaborative and educational nature of church:

We are urged to be participatory in decision making. That's why we have a voted-upon vestry to be representative of who we are as a people of our church. And I think it would be difficult and it would really require a lot of teaching.

This educational role and the benefits of collaborative efforts served priests and parishioners. In elaborating upon how she has evolved as a conflict negotiator, Fiona said she grew into the role of collaborative negotiator. The more she worked with members of her parish, the more she learned to trust them to resolve an issue together:

I didn't really appreciate that when you have people in the parish, wardens or vestry that you really trust, the importance of closing the door and saying: "I don't know how we're going to solve this, but we're not going to leave until we figure it out." You know and just sort of having the confidence to throw it back to the group. And you can't do that all the time, but sometimes it's really important.

While clergy expressed a clear need on their part to work collaboratively, this did not mean they were lacking in their own opinions concerning a desired outcome, nor did they acquiesce to collaborative approaches as a way of relinquishing responsibility and authority. There was a clear appreciation for the opinions of others, but that was balanced by an equal sense of determination. Osmond carefully outlined the collaborative steps he would take, but he was still quite adamant in his support for full inclusion of gays and lesbians within the church, saying:

Part of what I'd try to do as a parish priest is to separate the ideological from the theological. Too many people, in my judgment, assume that this homosexuality issue is a liberal cause. I happen to think as a raving, screaming, Anglo-Catholic conservative theological priest that this is a very conservative issue. The prophets are pretty damn clear on what ought to happen in the involvement with other people.

Another priest also worked consciously to remain balanced in the midst of assorted social interactions. Although he has a number of gay friends and is passionate in his support of gay rights, Harry said that he has learned to tread carefully in order to make room for a more collaborative approach. In his efforts to resolve related conflicts, he opened up the issue to the whole congregation, but also attempted to be especially sensitive to divergent views:

> The congregation called me to be the rector and they knew where I stand on these issues . . . and they know that I've been on the Board of the Oasis, which is the ministry that works with gay and lesbian people. Having said that, I'm not a heavy-handed guy. So I wouldn't want to just force it down people's throats, especially knowing that there's a big part of a tradition that's against it.

So Harry and others walked a fine line and had to utilize many skills as they balanced their views with those of the congregation. Clergy said that they had learned that collaborative efforts including listening, encouraging dialogue, and providing educational support for the community were among the most successful strategies. Much of this points to the importance of communication in efforts to bring about a collaborative resolution. The words of Connor, a seasoned urban priest, captured the sentiments of many:

> I would want to open the lines of communication. I would want to spend time working on what is the teaching of the Episcopal Church. And the long journey that we've taken in educating people and bringing people on board to being a progressive community.

In outlining the most successful conflict resolution strategies, collaborative efforts were often emphasized. For some clergy, the greatest learning experiences regarding conflict resolution came about through inclusive efforts. They attempted to communicate with and incorporate as many interested parties as they could into this process of mutual discovery leading to reconciliation. Yet this approach did not preclude learning from other individuals in different settings.

Collaboration with Role Models

About a third of the clergy mentioned role models. Intentionally or not, some appeared to channel the perspectives of their role models as they attempted to resolve their own conflicts. There were also similarities in temperament between the individual and the role model they described. Enthusiastic in his support of gay rights, Osmond described his role model as being an equally impassioned personality during race riots of the 1960s:

> Bob went down the middle of the street, arms up, saying "I want to sit down and talk about this." And also the Vietnam War was just starting to get some protests. I saw that and thought: Oh, that's the team I want to play for.

Calm and poised in her demeanor, Greta cited Gene Robinson, the first openly gay bishop within the Episcopal Church, as her role model:

> And as Eugene Robinson says about himself, he's the only *openly* gay bishop. I'm sure we have other gay bishops. And he's been a wonderful role model when you think how he has been attacked and he just keeps his cool.

In learning to accept her daughter's homosexuality, Greta found Bishop Robinson to be a great inspiration. Yet patterning one's own behavior on that of others was shown to present its own set of problems. Once again the issue of remaining balanced emerged. As Fiona said:

> I think that the trick for me has been that I've seen models of clergy that are either so collaborative they don't have any [laughter] they don't have any self! There's no direction. There's no leadership. Or I have seen clergy who are SO directive that there isn't really much room for collaboration because it is so autocratic.

Fiona admitted that it took time for her to grow into her own unique approach, one that she described as a hybrid collaborative leadership style.

Collaboration with Mentors

While only two priests spoke directly of mentors, they did so with a deep sense of appreciation. During the years when the ordination of gay clergy in the Episcopal Church was new and highly contested, a few bishops were known for their unwavering support and for the guidance they offered to priests in their diocese. Grant described his bishop as such a mentor:

> I also had a bishop who was just incredibly supportive. When he learned about the conflict in the parish, I didn't have to call him. He called me. He said, "What can we do

to help you?" And he's somebody with national horizon prominence and it was nice to know that if I needed to play a trump card I had it. He was known to come to vestry meetings . . . parish meetings, and he would come on the annual Episcopal visit and before he came he said, "What's hot in your parish?"

The accessibility and support of such mentors provided a strategically useful and supportive outlet. The supportive benefits associated with social learning were perhaps most evident when peer support groups were discussed.

Collaboration with Peers

Having a circle in which to vent and reveal genuine and unedited concerns contributed significantly to the learning process. Being able to test out new strategies in a nonjudgmental environment and receive feedback from those who had weathered a similar plight was discussed as being invaluable. Harry found a certain degree of camaraderie with fellow teachers at the school where he taught on a part-time basis. He also talked about his experiences with a supportive group of clergy whom he met with on a regular basis. When dealing with the most challenging of conflicts, he would share his experiences and bring his concerns to the group in order to elicit their input and suggestions.

> So yeah, a colleagues group was invaluable. It really was in helping me to wind my way through. Most of them were older than I and had many more years of ministry experience. So when I would come with my issue, they would smile and say, "Yep, we've been there."

For Harry, that simple acknowledgement meant a great deal. It helped to ease him through the difficult conflicts by knowing that others had been through similar storms and survived.

Learning from Past Experience

Repetition and exposure to new perspectives were key contributors to the learning process. Painful as it may have been, the experience of negotiating emotionally charged conflicts served as an experience that prepared clergy to resolve conflicts in subsequent situations. More than half of the individuals I interviewed emphasized the role of experience as it related to their ability to negotiate more effectively. Grant was emphatic and very clear in his mind that it was through past experience that he gained the skills and the confidence necessary to utilize conflict strategically.

> Experience is a piece of that, and every time one goes through one of these one is learning. I think I'm still learning. It becomes clear that you can survive it. In fact you can not only survive it, but it can be actually a very positive thing. Sometimes I confess I create conflict.

Grant was the only person who admitted to actively initiating conflict to achieve greater good. He was also one of the three clergy who received formal conflict resolution training. Conflict was not something most volunteered to experience. Some were quite direct in stating their dislike. Kelly's words reflected the sentiments of others when she said, "Well, it's always hard, I think. I really don't like conflict. I would go around the bush to avoid it." While most indicated they would not initiate it, more than half described critical incidents in which they learned to deal more effectively with conflicts precisely through the experience of negotiating a conflict. This was true regardless of whether the outcome had been successful or not.

Though she disliked conflict, Kelly made the observation that her approach to certain conflicts today would be much different based on her past experiences. She had, for example, learned a great deal through the experience of handling a conflict involving a gay parishioner who left her parish in response to an offensive joke about homosexuals told by a fellow parishioner. She said that she would now make more of an effort to educate the parishioner who had made the offensive remark than she had at the time. Humor, she pointed out, needed to be directed only at those who would not be hurt by it. As she said:

> We're supposed to be a community and support each other. . . . The point was we don't talk like that. If you want to make jokes, make them about the Hittites. They're all dead.

Surprisingly, Grant and others spoke of their experience negotiating conflicts as a confidence builder. It provided them with an additional set of tools, skills, and resources that helped minimize the conflict and allowed them to move toward a resolution with fewer insecurities. When they were able to truly embody the posture of a priest, their fears diminished. The more experience they had utilizing this model, the less overwhelmed they were when faced with new conflicts. As Fiona said:

> You know, I find that it helps, really it helps the longer
> I do this. At the beginning I was incredibly defensive
> because I was incredibly unsure of myself. . . . But I think
> that it also comes with experience where you feel better
> about yourself and in less, less in need of defending.

Although Harry, who described himself as an easy-going kind of guy, admitted to disliking conflict, he too learned to accept it. Time has helped him develop the skills needed to move through conflicts more effectively. "I'm learning more and more how to deal with it when I do have to have it. 'Cause you do have to have conflict," he said. When asked how he specifically learned to negotiate emotionally sensitive conflicts touching on some aspect of homosexuality, he attributed it to experience, saying:

> I think just doing it, by dealing with it, getting a thicker
> skin myself. It really has . . . helped. So I guess that just
> doing it, unfortunately.

Harry and others admitted that experience generated the most learning. They learned how to negotiate conflicts by going through the process of attempting to resolve them. Yet the value of experience surfaced in another way.

Loretta, Ellen, and Connie each reported that the more personal life experiences they were able to bring to the table the better. Broader life experiences contributed to their ability to resolve a variety of conflicts, including those dealing with homosexuality. They said that their experiences made them better able to accommodate, relate to, and understand a greater spectrum of perspectives. It also seemed that the greater the experience, the greater their capacity for compassion. Life experience appeared to widen their hearts.

Not only did such experiences expand their feelings and their thinking, it also seemed to boost their confidence levels. They grew increasingly comfortable and relaxed as they were able to examine conflicts from many sides (to frame and reframe the issues in a variety of ways), and as a result they became better negotiators. Two priests with distinctly different backgrounds expressed the importance of life experience as an educational resource.

According to Ellen, who was raised in an extremely conservative and strict military family and came of age during the 1960s, "The more educated you are, the more liberal you tend to be because you've had greater exposure." She had lived through a number of social movements, including those promoting gay rights, women's rights, and the struggle for racial equity. As she stated, "You know, I'm sixty-two years old. I've lived a very adventuresome life." She went on to discuss how her perspective had changed because of her exposure to so many experiences. As a result, she became more receptive to the perspective of others. "I have learned over time to be accepting of people."

At approximately the same time as Ellen, Loretta grew up at the other end of the geopolitical spectrum. She was raised in Berkeley, California, during this time of social change. She said that her early experiences in such a liberal environment helped her, in later years, to resolve a variety of conflicts. Exposure to liberal views she believed helped her move beyond the fear that sometimes generates conflict. She said:

> One of the things that is bottom line for me is broad experience. I think an awful lot of the fears of homosexuality, or the fear of race, or the fear of ethnicity, comes from a lack of experience. I was blessed to grow up in a place where one of the questions on the playground at school was: What do you speak at home? And if the answer was English, then you were considered to be a little less interesting.

She laughed as she admitted that she would have been one of those considered less interesting, but she was firm in her belief that those early experiences shaped her for the better. Connie also highlighted the value of a broad perspective based on life experience, which allowed her to better contextualize conflicts that arose within the church. In recounting her religious evolution, she said:

> I grew up Methodist and then became a real charismatic in college. Was Evangelical conservative. I was very Evangelical. Oh yeah man, I know the talk. I can do it. I was a missionary for eight years in Africa in Liberia, and in Bolivia. And I was a pediatric oncology nurse. And so when I came to priesthood, it was with a world of other experiences that have so molded my sense that this [the role of Christians] is much bigger than any church.

Here she was referring to current conflicts within the Episcopal Church over efforts to be more accepting of gays. The mission of Christ, as she perceived it, was the guiding force upon which she focused as she negotiated her way through conflicts in her own life and within the church. This focus enabled her to tread carefully as she attempted to resolve current conflicts with family members regarding homosexuality.

Greta spoke of past experience in a slightly different way. She identified it as a harbinger of change. She shared the story of how her views had shifted as she learned to accept homosexuality to such an extent that she was comfortable officiating at her daughter's commitment ceremony. She said she was convinced that exposure to a number of gays was evidence of God's movement in her life. By getting to know gay members of the clergy, for example, her perspective was widened. This she believed ultimately allowed her to resolve a long-standing conflict and fully accept her gay daughter.

Learning through experience took a number of forms. Through repeated attempts to resolve conflicts, clergy refined their skills. Breadth of life experiences allowed them to contextualize conflicts, minimize fears, and bring an open heart along with a broader perspective to negotiations. It was through multiple experiences that clergy learned to reconcile differences of opinion.

Observation of Role Models

The impact of observing others was spoken of as being quite powerful by one quarter of those I interviewed. Loretta recounted incidents where she observed the actions of her parents. She attributed her broad-minded views to what she described as their sense of "radical equality," which so dominated the behavior she observed as a child. So, for example, she said:

> I was raised that it was rude and dehumanizing to call people by anything other than by their first name, which meant that we didn't say mom and dad. We said Edgar and Lara, and it meant I called my father's Nobel Laureate colleagues Oscar and Ethan. I think that kind of teaching very early on was that we're all equal.

She said that she learned how to interact with others by observing this very particular life view demonstrated through the actions of her parents. It had a profound and lasting impact. She suggested that it was, in part, responsible for her view that whether gay or straight, individuals should be afforded the same rights. Her personal sense of "radical equality" was applied to all individuals regardless of race, ethnicity, socioeconomic status, or sexual identity.

Formal Learning

Training Programs

Only three priests had received any specific formal instruction designed to help them negotiate their way through conflicts, but none had received conflict resolution training in seminary. In fact, as Petra and others pointed out, many clergy had a tendency to avoid conflicts.

> Conflict resolution is always messy. . . . You have to be very courageous to go into conflict. There's very few, I don't know as you've been talking to people if anyone really says that's my charism, to go into conflict-ridden places and really submerge myself in conflict and really help them resolve. 'Cause most priests that I know really don't like it. And nobody wants to deal with it, but it's inevitable, especially in the church.

Grant, the only person who admitted that he had sometimes generated conflict to move an issue forward, received his conflict resolution training through the Industrial Areas Foundation (IAF), an organization involved in neighborhood citizen reform groups across America. The IAF understanding of the role of community organizers included the utilization of power bases to effect social change. As Grant described it:

> That's where I learned the value of a one-on-one interview with somebody where you're not trying to sell anybody anything. You're listening, and not trying to say you need to buy my idea. I'm going to try and see it the best I can as you see it. You don't have to agree with this, but we do have to listen to each other . . . as best we can. And you don't have to do it my way. So there's a lot of stuff that wasn't seminary training that I got along the way.

This training that enabled him to try to see things from the perspective of others was, in reality, teaching him to reframe the issues just as one is called to do by experts in conflict negotiation. This ability to reframe is a key component in the conflict resolution process.

Connor had also received training through the IAF program. While both he and Grant had resolved many conflicts over the course of their seasoned careers, and perhaps because they had lived through so many, they did not speak of approaching conflict with the same sense of dread that was described by other, less experienced clergy. Rather, in discussing their experiences, they projected an especially balanced sensibility. They were able to take a more clinical approach while at the same time being acutely aware of the feelings involved. As Connor said:

> I've been in the midst of conflict and tension over this issue [of gay rights]. But I was trained in community organizing by the Industrial Areas Foundation. . . . I will go back to my community organizing training. It's about feelings, and you have to get to a place where people can talk about their feelings. Because often times in the feelings there is not accurate data.

Both Grant and Connor believed that the training they received had refined their ability to focus on the pertinent details without drowning in a sea of information and emotions. So while they were trained in seminary to assume the posture of a priest and focus on a higher plane, it was the IAF training that provided them with the tools needed to remain on course during negotiations. Their formal training set them apart. For most it was a process of trial and error that incorporated a variety of individuals including congregants, role models, mentors, and peers. So while formal learning offered clear advantages, there was no shortage of less structured and equally illuminating learning opportunities for clergy to take advantage of.

Questions to Ponder

1. Who are the individuals that comprise my conflict support group? Or who are my role models, peers, mentors, etc. that I can turn to in my personal efforts to learn how to resolve conflicts?

2. When I look at conflicts I have negotiated in the past, if I were to model an arms out, palms open approach, how might my behavior have changed?

3. How have my past experiences shaped my approaches to conflict resolution?

4. Which experiences have had the most impact on shaping my approach?

CHAPTER 7

Seeing Conflict as a Spiritual Learning Tool

Panoramic View

To fully appreciate the ways in which clergy learned to negotiate difficult conflicts, it is important to examine their approaches from multiple perspectives to get a panoramic view. The effort to resolve conflicts over gay inclusion took on a larger meaning for many of those I interviewed. While chapter 6 examined how they went about learning to address the challenges, this chapter presents an analysis of the effectiveness of their methods from distinct yet overlapping perspectives.

The approaches utilized by clergy are first discussed from a Christian perspective. What do their actions tell us about the existence of a distinctly Christian approach to conflict resolution? It is also worth noting that many of the instinctive responses of the clergy I spoke with reflected not only a Christian worldview, but also an approach that incorporated the best of learning and negotiation strategies touted by experts in each field.

Clergy discussed and demonstrated through their actions that they worked hard to establish trust and facilitate dialogue. Experts in the field of conflict negotiation have pointed out that trust is an important bond and component that helps individuals to resolve conflicts with relative ease. The importance of effective communication skills is also emphasized. Many experts agree that while good communication has been identified as helpful, it alone does not eradicate conflict, but the absence of good communication skills can certainly inflame the situation and lead to a stalemate or worse.

Mindful of the many spheres in which they were operating, clergy accomplished their goals by moving forward with an overarching strategy that incorporated principles associated with Christianity, learning theorists, and conflict negotiators. While treading very carefully to resolve conflicts over gay inclusion, clergy ventured into these uniquely distinct areas.

Mingling Secular and Spiritual

To initiate the negotiation process and to be most effective, clergy first needed to become centered spiritually. Some, for example, discussed a spiritual practice that involved continual prayer, or time at a monastery. Secondly, as most were initially unschooled in the art of conflict negotiation, they were forced to devise a learning strategy. A few spoke of reading books to bring themselves up to speed and an even smaller number went through formalized training. Yet they all discussed the informal and social approaches to learning that they found invaluable. The third and final area they needed to confront was the actual process of negotiation. Spiritual matters, the process of learning, and the skills of a negotiator would, on the surface, appear to be very separate and distinct enterprises. Yet the approaches clergy utilized most successfully were often seamlessly interconnected.

Conflict Resolution Strategies Viewed through Assorted Lenses

Christian Lens

In examining the approaches taken by clergy to resolve difficult conflicts, I discovered that their Christian approach was guided by four general principles. There was a high regard for **communal engagement**, an appreciation of the need for personal growth through **spiritual development**, a need for **reflection,** and these efforts were grounded in an agape **love**. Many would agree that these elements are integral parts of a Christian ethos. Based in Christian doctrine, they also served as the backbone for the strategies clergy designed to resolve conflicts over gay inclusion.

Communal Engagement

Within Christianity there is a great emphasis on communal ties. There is the expectation that individuals come together for a greater good. The communal aspects of Christian life lead one quite naturally to examine the impact of social interactions within the community. Essential to all Christians regardless of their denominational affiliation, faith develops as individuals are in relationship with others. This inherent social obligation is part of the Christian way of life.

So it seems quite natural that clergy selected an approach to resolve the conflict that incorporated communal efforts. Some spoke quite openly of their acquired appreciation for a more interactive and social form of learning. They admitted that as they matured into the role of spiritual leader, they could more readily accept the fact that they did not have all the answers and could call on their community for support when in the midst of negotiating an especially emotionally charged conflict. This understanding allowed them to become more comfortable in adopting collaborative approaches to resolve conflicts. Collaboration grew out of confidence—a confidence in the community's ability to grapple with the issue, a confidence in their receptivity to the Holy Spirit, and a confidence in their understanding of their role within the various communities touched by the dispute. With confidence, fears abated.

As clergy tended to the multiple communities involved in the conflict, they learned that it was also important for them to recognize their own needs because they too were important members of the community. Self-care was vital if they were to continue being a useful member of the community. They needed to be tended to for their own personal welfare, but also in order to be of use to their social network. While they served others, they were also fed through communal efforts. More than one priest identified isolation as toxic and something to be avoided at all costs.

Appreciation for Personal Growth through Spiritual Development

Learning to resolve conflicts within this social milieu brought about the potential for both immediate and long-term benefits. There was the obvious gratification that comes with resolving a conflict, but there was also the potential for a deeper fulfillment that comes as one develops spiritual resilience. The communal approaches chosen by clergy as they negotiated conflicts had the added benefit of creating very concrete learning opportunities for spiritual growth.

Rather than simply eliminate or cover up the problems generated by the conflict, clergy often elected to use the problem for a larger purpose. The conflict became a tool that encouraged disputants to deepen their faith. So conflicts had the potential to take on a deeper level of meaning. By electing to wrestle with each of the difficulties that surfaced in highly emotional conflicts, their faith was tested in a number of ways. By negotiating conflicts like those over gay rights, both clergy and parishioners had the opportunity to develop spiritually.

Need for Reflection

When individuals are stuck in the middle of a conflict, reflection provides a space in which they can move beyond initial or limited viewpoints. In fact, the challenges of conflict resolution provide significant opportunities for learning through reflection. In the midst of resolving conflicts, negotiators are often called to reframe the issues being discussed. This process of reframing requires one to ponder and think and rethink the presentation of issues.

A number of the men and women I interviewed shared stories that incorporated their own reflective experiences. While bringing a depth of thought may contribute to the resolution of the conflict, in the midst of conflict, it is challenging to take time out to reflect. Grant, who with nearly forty years of ministry has weathered many conflicts, said:

> I think that in some ways that's what really happens in these conflict situations. One does the job and later on we learn. It's like John Lennon says, reality is that thing that's going on out there while we're talking about it in here. I think that's one of the pieces that is helpful about reflecting upon that experience.

Several priests began to have a change of heart concerning issues of gay inclusion during their seminary years as an event caused them to think about their beliefs. Through reflection, they were able to reframe the issues. Connie, for example, began to take a closer look at Scripture and reflect on the fact that she was getting to know deeply religious gay men and women for the first time. Although she came from a conservative background, her experience with other seminarians filled with the Holy Spirit, her study of the Bible, and ultimately her reflection on both experiences reshaped her understanding. Today, through additional experiences and reflection, she holds a much more liberal view. Now she struggles in her relationship with conservative family members, but she highlighted the importance and value of time.

Connie attributed some of the conflicts within the church to the feeling on the part of more conservative members that changes are being thrust upon them. She said she believes that people have simply not had the chance to catch up to the changes. This view was reinforced by Fiona and others.

Not only did clergy I interviewed value reflection, they also encouraged a reflective response from others involved in conflict negotiations. Given their contemplative nature and formal training in seminary that encourages reflection upon theological concerns, it is not surprising that it was embedded in their approach to dealing with day-to-day matters as well. Serving as educators, clergy were responsible for helping others move forward as learners. Many clergy took on the role of both educator and facilitator as they led and encouraged disputants in order to reach resolution. Connor, for example, who had received significant training in community organizing, admitted to taking an active role in encouraging others to reflect.

> I understand a little bit about power dynamics and organizing and so I'm trying to work through things and help people sort it out. So my usual way of dealing with stuff is that I put something out on the table and I give people time to think about and process it. And I say we need to make a decision and I'm even willing to say that the decision is in place for 120 days or 180 days and then we come back.

By providing the congregation with an experience that included time to reflect on the issues surrounding the conflict, and allowing them to even revisit and perhaps reframe their view, Connor assumed the role of educator-facilitator. When individuals are learning through experience, educators may play a vital role by challenging learners to develop new perspectives regarding the situation by encouraging them to reframe that experience.

Unlike some denominations, the Episcopal Church encourages parishioners to bring a thoughtful perspective. It does not have a literalist tradition that equates the Bible with science. In discussing the difference between Episcopalians and those from a more literal Protestant background, Loretta likened it to the tale of *The Runaway Bunny*. In this 1942 classic children's story by Margaret Wise Brown, a playful baby bunny tries to run away from home and transforms into other creatures and objects in order to hide. On each occasion the loving mother bunny transforms herself into an object in order to bring her baby bunny back home. At one point in the story, the baby rides the waves to escape and his ears are transformed into sails. Later, as he threatens to fly away, his ears are transformed into wings and so on. In making an analogy, Loretta said:

> You don't read *The Runaway Bunny* to learn about rabbit physiology. You don't read Genesis to learn how the earth was formed. And as thinking people that's pretty much the way Episcopalians understand things. A literalist fundamentalist interpretation is really a pretty modern thing. It was a backlash to the Enlightenment. It never really got set until the early nineteenth century. So if you want to think like early nineteenth century, go right ahead.

For Loretta, overarching intellectual acts of reflection were an integral part of the Episcopal Church and an aspect that she valued highly.

Efforts Grounded in Love

Love provided a foundation that allowed clergy to open their arms and their hearts as they moved through conflict negotiations. Caring for others involved communal efforts that fostered individual spiritual growth. For clergy this included becoming vulnerable and being the one willing to place something on the negotiation table first. The love that enabled them to do so took many forms, and it was certainly not a weak and passive love. Rather, there was great power in strategies grounded in love.

By naming the AIDS ministry the Ministry of Love, Ellen's church took a powerful stand. Osmond's unequivocal welcome of an estranged gay parishioner who wept upon being accepted back into the church spoke to the power of an inclusive love. Love also had the power to melt hardened hearts. With time, Carole's homophobic in-laws came to love her closest gay friend. Greta described how her heart softened as she developed relationships with gay clergy that ultimately led to her acceptance of a lesbian daughter.

Yet love was not always pretty and, as Connor suggested, some priests shied away from a tougher form of love out of a fear of their parishioners' anger. In his view, pushing parishioners, just as one pushes one's children, was a necessary part of his job. It required discipline and was not always easy to do. There were times when it also required drawing a line in the sand. Grant experienced this firsthand in what was one of the most difficult moments in nearly forty years of ministry. Following his church's establishment of an AIDS center, he was compelled to tell a parishioner she would need to find another place of worship after she loudly snapped on latex gloves during Communion.

Love wore many faces and brought many challenges. Yet it was most commonly demonstrated by clergy through consistency. Harry continues to visit and minister to the parishioner who left his church following an angry outburst at gays in response to a sermon given by a gay seminarian. Peter did not leave the Episcopal Church after parishioners literally turned their back on him and a bishop refused to bless him. In fact, it was experiences such as these that strengthened their ability to minister unto others.

Adult Learning Lens

Appropriate Choices

In both structured and unstructured environments, real life can serve as the ultimate learning laboratory. There is an increasing appreciation for informal modes of learning, as they can provide a lasting impact and be shaped to accommodate a variety of needs. Clergy held a dual role with regard to learning. First, they often served as educators helping others wrestle with difficult issues and emerge with some degree of wisdom. Secondly, they were engaged in their own struggles to gain insights through their personal life experiences. So they were both educators and learners. In addition, as individuals who had attended seminary, each of them had successfully moved through formal learning experiences. Yet the clergy I interviewed repeatedly selected informal modes of learning in order to develop their conflict negotiating skills.

As clergy were very interested in communal engagement, spiritual development, and reflection, it was the informal modes of education that were particularly well suited to their goals. Their choices encouraged participation from members of their community, allowed for reflection, and ultimately facilitated spiritual growth. In the end, the various forms of interactions with others led to visceral experiences that made lasting impressions and brought about change.

Social Learning through Social Networks

Learning often occurs in relation to a social context. Because the social environment can play a significant role in the learning process, it is important to examine the behavior of those within that social environment. Social learning theorists argue that individuals construct new ways of operating based in part on their observation of others. In fact, it is widely accepted that the learning process would be extremely tedious, and in some instances quite dangerous, if we had to invent each experience without having the benefit of observing others. So we often model our behavior on the actions of others in our various social networks.

The individuals that clergy observed within their social circles included role models, peers, and mentors. These were some of the influential persons with whom clergy were associated during their efforts to negotiate conflicts. Just as influential persons make an impact on clergy, clergy members themselves, through their interactions with others within their parish, for example, influence those around them. Learning thus becomes an essential part of communal life. Clergy often found that learning to resolve conflicts was best achieved through some interactive process.

As Ellen said, when faced with resolving conflicts, "Don't sit in your office and make up rules." The effort to maintain social interactions, even when it was difficult to do so, was viewed as an important element in the resolution process. Osmond saw firsthand how social interactions within a community of believers could move people past their initial biases. He saw a shift take place within his parish because of continuous interactions. During the early years of the AIDS crisis, one flamboyant, interracial gay couple came to be embraced by members of a very conservative parish. It was a slow process, but the couple persevered in spite of the unlikelihood of acceptance. Osmond said that they "by their sheer personality won people over."

> When one of them died, I had a full church on a weekday.
> I had a full choir. The choir took personal days off from
> work. When we processed out from the church into the
> columbarium, the whole congregation was there. And so
> I began to see that personal contact can make a difference.

He also saw how learning grew out of social interactions. In a different incident, following an impromptu meeting between a visiting bishop from the Sudan and a group of gay priests, the absence of contact led to misconceptions. An informal gathering was arranged in the midst of an annual conference for priests.

> It wasn't heralded. It was just a quiet little . . . in a little
> room with about a dozen people. And he did come out
> of there saying, "These are good people. I did not know."
> He was admitting to our bishop that he hadn't met a gay
> person. Between you and me he had! He just didn't know
> it. So it was, here we are in the twenty-first century. He's

having this first experience of realizing that they actually can talk like other people. So the personal is powerful if it's conducted with an attempt to hear rather than an attempt to convert, proselytize.

Yet the social context was also sometimes perceived as an impediment to the learning process, preventing those in conflict from moving forward. In discussing an experience that seemed unrelated to conflicts over homosexuality, Connie spoke of her time in a Virginia church within a segregated community. Parishioners wondered why African-Americans in the community felt uncomfortable walking up the steps to their church. To Connie the reason seemed clear. It was white, pre-Revolutionary, and the surrounding cemetery was filled with Confederate markers. She joked that she and the other rector secretly plotted to tear down the large Confederate statue in front of the church. Yet she saw parallels between divisions within the Virginia church over race and divisions within the larger Episcopal Church over issues of gay inclusion. She said:

> On that issue, on sexuality, I think these issues are very connected. Because we want our church to be like us. I don't want anything that's going to make me uncomfortable. I want a comfortable faith with people who are like me, who understand the Gospel like me.

She found this to be a common, disturbing, and divisive perspective within some religious circles. For her it was not the role of Christians to simply seek out the status quo and limit their sense of community. She did not feel called simply to manage comfort and sameness. As Peter said, "Conflict. It's your job to lead people through it. It comes with being a priest." This belief that managing conflict is part of their responsibility is understandable, as clergy members often see themselves as the caretakers of their local religious communities.

Care for their communities also necessitated that they provide learning opportunities for the members. Priests often spoke of these opportunities as being social in nature. They could not force learning, but factors like proximity, frequency of contact, and level of respect for behavioral models can have an impact on the individual learner. Ultimately, however, each person serves as his or her own gatekeeper in a self-regulatory process that sometimes takes one down a long and winding path strewn with surprises along the way.

Greta, a priest in her seventies, was raised with the idea that marriage could only exist between a man and a woman. She grew up at a time and within a family setting where certain aspects of sexuality were simply never discussed. She admitted that she was at least sixteen before she even learned the word "homosexual." People just did not speak of it, she said. Yet over time she experienced a personal evolution regarding her views on homosexuality. The shift was gradual and initially occurred within the context of her workplace. In the 1970s, a gay curate came to their church. Years later when her rector died, a lesbian priest held another position in their church. With increased exposure came acceptance. Greta became friends with the priest and her partner and attributed the gradual attrition of opposition to homosexuality to these and other social relationships with gay men and women.

By the time of her own daughter's coming out as a lesbian, Greta admitted that her attitude toward homosexuality had already begun to shift. Though she did not initially embrace the idea, it was social interactions that had paved the way toward her acceptance. Greta also drew a parallel between her spiritual maturation and her ability to fully accept her daughter as gay. For her, social learning was integrally connected to her spiritual development. Greta said she believed God strategically placed gays and lesbians in her life as a way of broadening her understanding of humanity. She was quite definitive and said:

> Yes, I think my spiritual development advanced and my understanding of our being made in the image of God. And that we're all human beings. And that there ought not to be any difference between us.

Social learning sometimes allows for exposure and contact with those outside of our comfort zone and can certainly be linked to the spiritual development process. Neither journey is one of isolation. Human interactions contribute to both the spiritual maturation and the adult learning process. We develop spiritually as we interact with one another and our learning is also augmented through interactive experiences.

Learning through Lasting Experiences
Experiences not only stick with us, they can alter our behavior and future actions. Our perspectives are significantly shaped through our experiences, and we are in a sense the sum total of all our encounters. Experiential learning emanates from visceral experiences that lead to changes of behavior. It involves working out solutions to real-life situations firsthand. So if learning is likened to a bridge that links the

known with the unknown, then experiential learning is the vehicle that enables us to cross that bridge. We are able to take the next step in part because of the cumulative nature of experiential learning. Ideas are developed and modified through experiences in the social world as we test them out. While we may face new situations, we approach them with the cumulative experiences that we have amassed over the course of our lives.

For clergy I interviewed, social experiences provided a type of learning that individual or solitary experiences did not. In describing what he learned as he emerged from a personal crisis that was to some degree managed in a social sphere, one priest spoke of learning through the experience of suffering. Going through a public and protracted divorce led to a series of inner conflicts as well as a number of conflicts within his parish. As Osmond confessed:

> I had this expectation that I was supposed to be perfect. And many, if not most, clergy people have a struggle with that issue. I'm supposed to set an example. I'm supposed to be a role model. And then, I learned a human role model shows you how to learn through suffering. It took probably twenty years on this side of suffering to be able to say this as calmly as this. Because my own expectation of me, of prayer, of life—that had all been shattered. So I had to work my way through theological immaturity and silly priestly identity, and I discovered that recognizing that I'm flawed enabled me to be more pastorally accepting in others.

Osmond went on to say that the experience of suffering in this deep and public way also made him much more sensitive to the gay world. The bruising and scars he weathered, along with the support he received from his bishop, sensitized him to the needs and suffering of others, including gays and lesbians within his congregation and family. For him the parallel between how he was treated within his community and how he should ideally treat others was clear.

Moving through this very real learning experience forced Osmond to confront expectations of himself and others. In the end, he managed to resolve this personal conflict that was played out in a very public, or social, arena. As a result of the experience, he was changed, as were his subsequent interactions with individuals from multiple communities.

Experiences also offered visceral learning opportunities for Grant. In describing his fifteen years as a volunteer firefighter, he explained that while they received a great deal of training, and while they were provided with the most advanced technical equipment, those were not the most important aspects of safety. Being retrofitted with good gear was of value, but as he pointed out, "What one learns quickly is, with whom one will risk." He said that there were always four or five fire-fighters who looked for one another when they arrived on the scene. They were the ones who went in together. It did not take many experiences for him to learn that the young and overly enthusiastic fire-fighter, who was crazed and would stay in too long, was not the best team member. A base of knowledge amassed through such memorable life experiences was invaluable.

Clergy generally learned to resolve conflicts over gay inclusion based on their experiences. Within the Episcopal Church there is no formal program that all clergy must complete in order to deal effectively with a number of conflicts and related practical matters. In reality no narrowly focused formal training could sufficiently prepare clergy for the range and nature of conflicts that exist within the church today. Just as no firefighting manual could provide the same visceral experience Grant had when going into a burning building with "hot shot" firefighters, no religious manual alone could prepare a new priest or deacon for the emotional strain of being at the epicenter of a difficult conflict resolution.

A number of clergy I interviewed attended seminary more than twenty years ago. Dramatic attitudinal shifts have occurred in society at large with regard to a variety of social issues, especially within the last decade. These unanticipated shifts have led to adjustments, accommodations, and conflicts within the church. Thus, the learning process for clergy should be seen as part of an ongoing form of engagement through experience. When change within a society is swift, reliance upon past experiences alone to negotiate the present is insufficient. Individuals are forced to continuously review their ideas and experience in the light of new and changing information. Thus it becomes a cyclical process of renewal.

Past experiences can prepare one to better assess and prepare for future experiences. In recounting a painful conflict in which one of his parishioners verbally attacked gay members of his church during a parish forum, Harry, a very mild-mannered person, said he learned to deal with conflicts of this kind by developing a thicker skin. This came through his experience of going through the process. He reluctantly admitted that it was only by experiencing the conflict that he learned to deal with it more effectively. While he was one of those who, if given the choice, would actively avoid conflict, he did come to expect it and saw it as necessary for both his individual and the congregational growth.

Harry also admitted that he is able to draw on the strength and experience of others. In the midst of one parish's struggle following the comments of a visiting and outspoken lesbian seminarian, Harry admitted that having a group of seasoned priests he could turn to helped significantly.

> Just from their experience, they're consoling me that I did a good job, saying: "Yes, that's happened to us also. Your responses were typical." I want to hear that I didn't screw it up totally. Yes, I'm a sensitive guy and I want to do a good job. . . . So I can share with them. . . . It definitely helped me.

Harry looked to more experienced priests for not only support but also for guidance. By gaining insights from their experiences, he was able to find his way through the complexities of the conflicts he was called to resolve.

The nature of current struggles within the Episcopal Church calls for an approach that allows for a variety of complexities. The learning that emanates from experiential learning incorporates a holistic approach that engages the learner on many levels. Rather than focusing on a fixed end point, it allows for and encourages a process of renewal. Individuals learn from their experiences as they reflect upon them. New experiences that affect their perspective occur and the process continues. Our environment and our collection of experiences as social beings continue to shape our point of view in an evolutionary process.

Negotiator's Lens

Conflict as a Positive Force

Current thinking in conflict resolution offers a useful model for the Church. A contemporary view sees conflict as an opportunity for growth and parallels the Christian understanding that spiritual development emanates from individual and collective struggles. Clergy, albeit sometimes reluctantly, recognized there was potential good to be found in the midst of conflict. As discussed previously, they appreciated the fact that conflict when managed and negotiated appropriately could lead to personal growth and spiritual development. This applied to their own as well as the disputants' enrichment. The potential they saw in conflict reflected a shift seen in the field of conflict studies itself.

Early approaches to conflict resolution were far more restrictive and viewed conflict as a problematic condition that required a fix. The more contemporary understanding places conflict at the very center of learning opportunities for both the individual and the organization in which the conflict is being resolved. When organizations view the inherent complexities of conflict as opportunities, there is the potential for growth. As a practical matter, it is not always possible or even desirable to eliminate conflict. So the real challenge then becomes how to resolve conflicts in ways that enhance individuals and organizations without rendering harm. Within a religious sphere, conflict can take on added value when it leads to spiritual growth. Since conflict is an inevitable feature of social and organizational life, it seems prudent to devise strategies that allow us to utilize it—organizationally or personally—in some positive way.

Contemporary theories of conflict resolution point out that conflict need not be approached with fear. Clergy too came to this realization and with time they were able to release the apprehension when called to resolve conflicts. Their initial views seemed to mirror early views in the field of conflict studies that seemed to exacerbate a sense of dread. Emphasis was on the tensions that existed between polar opposites. These models often sought a restoration of some idealized sense of order. In such scenarios, conflict was viewed as a harmful force, a negative experience that needed to be eradicated. Achieving the desired change was of greater importance than the journey itself. Conflicts were seen as something dangerous to be avoided at all costs.

On the other hand, contemporary views embrace the complexity and utilize conflicts to facilitate learning. There are those, for example, who believe that conflict within an intellectual environment provides fuel for learning. From this perspective, conflict is seen as a positive force that allows us to develop our resilience in any number of areas.

Conflict Resolution as a Learned Behavior
Even clergy who did not shy away from conflict admitted that the process of resolving conflicts was a learned behavior that required the development of specific skills. Experts agree that a full complement of knowledge, skills, and attitudes are required for the constructive resolution of conflicts. Certainly a broad-based strategy of adaptation and flexibility is called for. Negotiators must be responsive to the needs of

disputants and should design a strategy uniquely tailored to each individual situation.

The clergy I interviewed almost instinctively recognized the need to personalize their response. So, for example, they were cognizant of the fact that while open and heartfelt discussions may have helped to resolve conflicts in one situation with one group of people, such open-ended discussions could actually bring harm in another situation. While there were helpful guidelines they mapped out for themselves, there was no one template that could be used to address all subsequent conflict negotiations. While there are many approaches taken by conflict negotiators, certain strategies are especially well suited to certain types of conflict. A negotiator may take any number of effective approaches and there may be as many routes to the resolution as there are problems. The key is to be able to adapt to the individual situation.

It is true, however, that disputes that relate to our values, those ideas we hold as irrefutable truths, are among the most difficult to resolve. In instances where individuals are engaged in moral conflicts, they are less likely to exhibit flexibility. It is also more difficult for those in conflict over values to assume the perspective of those with whom they are in conflict. It becomes especially challenging to reframe the issues. These types of conflict pose the greatest challenges to negotiators. In fact, often disagreements over closely held beliefs are not fully resolved.

Current conflicts between members of the Episcopal Church and within the greater Anglican community involve struggles over beliefs. In such instances when it is anticipated that the disputants will continue to have some form of an interdependent relationship following the conflict, as is the case with those within the Anglican Communion, reconciliation is the most desired form of resolution. Reconciliation helps create a climate whereby long-term cooperation is likely.

These types of social conflicts—those that involve identities and attitudes like the current disagreements within the Episcopal Church—are some of the thorniest of conflicts to resolve. Tied to fundamental theological perspectives, these conflicts go well beyond the interpretation of documents. The view of some conservatives in opposition to gay rights is that the theology of those in support of gay inclusion is unrecognizable as Christianity. When beliefs are so dramatically polarized, conflicts become especially difficult to resolve. In these and other circumstances, the process is not necessarily intuitive, but one that must be learned. And regardless of whether it is for personal or for organizational growth, dealing effectively with conflict first requires a willingness to learn. While such learning may take place in any number of venues, there are some basic strategies that are useful in a variety of settings and in the negotiation of a number of different types of conflicts.

According to many experts, the essential steps involved in the negotiation of conflicts include establishing goals, devising strategies, and defining the issues. The ability to purposefully consider an event or experience contributes to the learning process and is vital. Such framing of a conflict situation is an essential component in defining the issues. As one reconsiders, one may then begin to reframe the situation, expand one's perspective, and bring about a resolution. In contrast, holding onto a narrow vision decreases the likelihood of reaching resolution and inhibits progression toward a resolution. In the process of stepping into the perspective of another person, through the framing and reframing of issues, we are essentially learning to think differently.

Framing and Reframing Situations
The ability to frame and reframe the issues within a conflict is a key step toward a successful outcome. In this process individuals define the issues as they deconstruct what is before them in order to make better sense of the situation. Within the context of conflict negotiation, framing entails identifying the key factors—those of greatest importance. There are many types of frames and each yields a different outcome. While it seems like basic effort, it can be quite a profound enterprise, as framing and reframing situations call for a questioning of our own personal assumptions.

At times we are all reluctant to let loose of the perceptions we hold as truths. Yet doing so can be liberating. As clergy learned to reframe the conflict situation they were called to resolve, new approaches to the problem emerged. This in turn helped negotiations move forward constructively. Framing and reframing the issues also has the added benefit of slowing down the process. One cannot change one's thinking overnight. The expanded time allowed clergy to tread carefully across potentially explosive terrain. They did not relinquish all beliefs, but they did entertain the possibility of understanding the situation from another perspective.

This willingness to take on the perspective of those on the opposite side of the table also conveys a willingness to really listen to their concerns. This was demonstrated by many people I interviewed, including Fiona. Though she has resisted being defined as a "gay priest," she is gay, out, and supports gay rights. While she views church efforts to fully include gays as a progressive move, she also spoke of a need to empathize with conservative Episcopalians who oppose such moves.

Fiona said that at times she has imagined how conservatives have perceived the sweeping changes. Especially concerning Anglicans in the Sudan, she believed that theirs was an especially complex situation and they needed to be given more time. Her willingness to bring in the many factors that shaped their opinion allowed her to reframe the situation and offer added empathy for those with whom she disagreed.

Dennis discussed a humorous exchange he once had with a conservative bishop concerning the role of women. Dennis had lived through many changes within the Episcopal Church, including the 1979 Prayer Book, the *Hymnal 1982,* as well as the ordination of women. He was also quite passionate in his support for some of the more controversial changes. He spoke of a heated discussion with bishops and priests in his diocese at the time when women were becoming fully accepted in leadership roles. In this public forum, he offered a reframing of the situation that challenged the conservative view. During a meeting in 1974, members of the clergy opposed to the ordination of women were voicing their opinion. Quite animated even as he recalled events, Dennis told me:

> One priest got up and said that Jesus did not have women followers! I asked if him if was Jewish and he said: "Of course not. Why would you ask that?!" I said, "Well Jesus had only Jewish men that became our first disciples." And he was insulted. But to me that made sense.

In discussing another situation, Osmond likened the importance of broadening a disputant's perspective through reframing to marital sexual relations. When counseling couples, Osmond indicated that they would sheepishly admit that their most wonderful moments of physical intimacy were times when they had shifted their perspective and placed their partner's sexual desires ahead of their own. That ability and willingness to assume the perspective of the other person was something he deemed to be of utmost importance in other social interactions.

Osmond's own perspective on gays and of homosexuality began to shift when he made friends with two men in seminary that he later learned were a gay couple. He was able to take what had been at the time a shocking discovery, and subsequently see the conflict from both sides of the issue—through the eyes of gays as well as conservative straight parishioners. To reframe, to let go of our own assumptions for a moment and take on the perspective of those sitting across from us at the negotiation table, calls for a certain amount of reflection.

Many theorists agree that the type of reframing required for a shift in thinking does not happen overnight. This is something Fiona experienced with her elderly parishioner-friend and Carole experienced with her in-laws. Time gave them all the space in which to reflect, to take in a new perspective and move forward in their reconciliations. It takes time to experiment with new realities and modify our point of view. Conflict negotiators attempt to make sense of an often complex set of events. The goal is to bring clarity to the situation and offer new approaches that help move parties forward in their discussions.

In some instances clergy consciously reframed their thinking. In other instances their experiences caused them to look at a situation differently. In resolving congregational conflicts, Fiona noted that it had taken years for her to be comfortable incorporating new perspectives when confronted with a problem. As a young priest in a new parish, she admitted to being defensive and overreactive. She cringed as she recalled an experience in which she responded to an especially vitriolic parishioner who challenged her choice of time for church services. Finally, on one occasion after a difficult encounter, Fiona told her, "That's what I said. That's what we'll do and that's what it is." She was responding to being attacked and lashed out with a level of self-importance that in the end she knew was inappropriate.

Yet through this experience she was able to not only understand what she had done wrong, but to behave differently in the future. She has learned to reframe her perspective particularly in pressured situations where she does not have all the information needed to make a decision. She noted that just a few days earlier, when a woman accosted her in front of the choir, acolytes, and ushers just moments before the 10:30 service, she was not distressed. The parishioner was upset about a decision made in the previous year during a vestry meeting the woman had not attended. Rather than be swept up in her fury, Fiona thought:

> I don't know what that's about, but it doesn't belong to me. . . .
> Seven or eight years ago I would have been in my office
> agonizing about it.

But experience, she said, had allowed her to view the situation much differently and thereby apply a different frame. She was able to reach back into her memory banks for a useful comparison, become centered, and then respond from a calmer, more generous place of love rather than fear.

Questions to Ponder _____

1. In what ways might I be able to use conflict negotiations to foster my own spiritual growth as well as the growth of individuals I am in conflict with?

2. If those around me were modeling their behavior on my current conflict negotiation style, what would be the most dominant behavior they would observe?

3. How would I frame, reframe, and reframe again the perspective of one of the most combative disputants in a conflict I negotiated in the past, and take an increasingly empathetic point of view with each reframing?

4. How might I apply these strategies when engaging in conflicts on a national or global level?

Part 5 | What It All Means for Clergy and for Us

A S THEY MOVED through difficult negotiations, and while it was not their intention, clergy nonetheless created a road map for others resolving a variety of difficult conflicts. The conclusions and recommendations that follow may help pave the way for continued learning and discussions as we each develop in our ability to successfully negotiate conflicts.

CHAPTER 8

Surveying the Distance Traveled

Summary/Questions

In sharing their experiences, clergy spoke about what they learned, the challenges they faced, and how they learned to be successful in resolving conflicts. Additional questions for consideration along with key points raised by clergy are included in this chapter.

What Clergy Learned by Assuming the Posture of a Priest

What is the most visible evidence of the values that I bring to the negotiation table as I attempt to resolve a conflict?

> Much of what clergy learned comes back to the attitude conveyed by the posture of a priest with arms out, palms open. As reluctant as they might have been to initiate the process, they were the strongest and most successful when they were receptive and vulnerable to the very circumstances they were called to resolve. Once they adopted a position of unconditional love, they were able to let go of the fear.

How do I demonstrate my support for those with whom I am in conflict?

> For an overwhelming majority, the posture of a priest included placing an emphasis on reaching out to provide a variety of forms of support for the entire community throughout the conflict negotiations. These supports ranged from respecting elected representatives of the parish enough to incorporate their perspectives into the resolution process, to nurturing individual parishioners. The majority of clergy had an initial response that included reaching out to those within the church hierarchy. Yet they also supported the congregation-at-large by reaching out in the form of offerings such as educational forums, lectures, and small discussion groups.

What and who makes up my safety net? Where and how do I receive the most support?

> In addition to outreach, the importance of an inner reach was acknowledged. Clergy had a clear recognition that support for themselves was vital. Recognizing the emotional stress they were under was the first step toward obtaining the emotional and spiritual support needed for them to withstand negotiations that were at times especially debilitating.

What skills do I need to refine in order to negotiate conflicts with an arms out, palms open approach?

> Assuming the posture of a priest also involved developing a very specific set of skills that were effectively utilized during the conflict negotiations. Many of these skills helped to support effective communication. The ability to listen actively, facilitate dialogue between the various parties, and patience were discussed as being especially helpful in creating a climate conducive to the resolution of the conflict. (See chapter 3.)
>
> Driven by a call for compassion, many emphasized the importance of inclusiveness. While this was linked to the call for social justice by some, a few felt that a focus on gay issues served to distract the church from a wider

social justice mission that included equally, or in some cases more, important issues. (See chapter 3.)

What are the ways I manage sameness within my own life rather than step out in faith to meet new challenges?

Having gay friends, coworkers, or relatives also appeared to sensitize clergy to the issues in a new way. The majority of clergy had personal and, in some cases, admittedly transformational relationships with gay men and women. These relationships were described as having had a bearing on their ability to resolve conflicts that touched on some aspect of gay inclusion. A shift in thinking took place in direct response to contact with gays. These changes were not immediate. They took place over a considerable amount of time. While other factors such as prayer or interpretation of Scripture surfaced, it was the establishment of personal relationships that was discussed as leading to tangible modifications of previously held beliefs as demonstrated by new behavior.

How the Challenges They Faced Were Best Addressed by Focusing on a Higher Plane

What are the primary competing interests that I need to accept as ambiguities and then temporarily set them to the side in order to focus on the priorities?

The majority of clergy sought to manage the dichotomy between pastoral and personal concerns on both an institutional and an emotional level. They were able to maintain a balanced approach only when they focused on a higher plane and avoided the pull to become overwhelmed by the many challenges.

The challenges presented on the institutional level were long-standing and deeply ingrained in the fabric of the Episcopal Church. While clergy and parishioners alike are called to utilize their reasoning capacity to determine church authority, they are also called to respect tradition as well as Scripture. These seemingly conflicting responsibilities challenge all within the Episcopal Church, even before attempts are made to resolve conflicts over any other matters.

In addition to managing institutional tensions, there were also inner, personal strains. A tension between personal and pastoral responses surfaced on an emotional level. Clergy were called to balance their personal reactions, preferences, and needs with responses that reflected the idealized response of a priest with arms out, palms open. By focusing on a higher plane, they were able to interact more effectively with the community involved in the conflict. Clergy were most successful when they prioritized and did not become distracted by the many challenges.

How They Learned to Tread Carefully

What fears do I bring when called to negotiate conflicts?

One of the most surprising discoveries to surface was the fact that few had received any training to deal with, let alone manage conflicts effectively. Given the number and nature of the conflicts members of the clergy are routinely called upon to resolve, I imagined that they would have received some type of training along the way. This was not the case. Initially this lack of preparation left many feeling hindered, apprehensive, and afraid. Yet through informal and social modes of learning, they came to understand that a safety net was in place and that improvements came only through repeated attempts. With this recognition, their fears were diminished.

If learning through experience serves as one of the greatest teachers, then why am I afraid to step out into the experience of conflict resolution?

Experiential learning led more than half of the men and women I spoke with to develop a better understanding of how to resolve conflicts effectively. For many it was a matter of trial-and-error experiences that taught them the most. They learned by doing and doing again with modifications based on what they had learned through each experience. In addition, the sheer experience of living enhanced their ability to resolve conflicts.

Many suggested that because of their unique experiences, they were better able to interact with a wide array of individuals and to empathize with a variety of individuals holding different perspectives. Some were exposed to diversity because of their geographic environment, others because they had come of age during a time of social upheaval. Many expressed a feeling that their exposure to a wide array of individuals and circumstances also made them better negotiators. In the end, as they came to understand and appreciate the cumulative benefits of experience as it related to their role as negotiators, they were less likely to approach conflicts with fear.

Making Sense of Their Experiences

Making Sense of What They Learned

In their conflict resolutions, clergy often asked questions to help reframe the issues. They looked for ways to emphasize common ground. They generally managed to control their emotions. They set aside a personal need to win in favor of elevated, long-term goals. They respected their "opponents." In fact, they did not label those involved in the conflict in such negative terms.

Clergy also, albeit painfully, recognized that sometimes one encounters individuals who are fueled by conflict to such a degree that reasonable efforts cannot counter their apparently insatiable appetite for disagreement. In such instances clergy recognized that it would not be possible to journey on with these individuals. The debilitating nature of such encounters underscored the importance of *not* being consumed by the conflict situation.

Yet of all that they learned, perhaps the most valuable lesson from a Christian perspective was that they could indeed step out in faith to resolve a variety of conflicts. While fear may have been the poison that prevented them from even attempting to succeed as a negotiator, love was the ultimate antidote.

Love allowed clergy to truly listen even when it was difficult to do so. When listening from an arms out, palms open stance, fears were more likely to be heard and subsequently addressed. Creating a space in which another person's feelings were acknowledged moved negotiations forward significantly. In fact, as Connor said, "often times in the feelings there is not accurate data." Yet the data may never even be shared in a hostile environment. So creating a more conducive climate was another key to success.

Making Sense of How They Learned

Irrespective of the training they received, clergy came to understand that reframing their perspectives, and helping others to reframe their individual perspectives as well, was a key and necessary step in the learning process. The ability to reframe is in fact a very empathetic act, as one is taking on another person's perspective.

In addition, the tension between what clergy felt they should do, and what the environment pushed them to do, helped propel them forward. This interplay prompted not only momentum but also a particular type of learning through an ongoing social-experiential-reflection cycle. Their reservoir of strategies was expanded as they moved through this learning cycle.

The nature and expectations associated with their role as religious leaders also demanded a thoughtful and balanced response. Hiding was not an option, and yet this too may have contributed to the learning process. The immediacy of the conflict situation almost forced them to learn. As they were unable to ignore the problem, they needed to construct a meaningful response. While immediacy can serve as a great motivator, individuals are also propelled into learning in response to a notable event. In fact, learning that truly transforms is often preceded by a jarring or disorienting quandary that causes one to adjust expectations or understandings.

The men and women I interviewed learned to question themselves and subsequently others as they experienced their own disorienting dilemmas. As their expectations of the world were disturbed, they were also able to help others learn to expand their perspectives.

This transformative nature of learning is especially apparent in Osmond's experience. It began with the discovery that his close seminary friends were a gay couple. He described his shock, but also discussed how he then visited Greenwich Village in New York City, just a few blocks south of his seminary. Though he admitted to recoiling at seeing two men display affection for one another, he came to accept that God's love is an inclusive love. He also said that even at the time he recognized that the range of emotions he felt was useful—it allowed him to be more empathetic toward those with homophobic tendencies. It was all so new at the time. Having experienced difficulty accepting the new reality before him, he said he could understand how others might find it difficult to accept new realities. So the experiences widened his perspective through several different frames.

Osmond's experience was very much akin to transformative learning experiences. He was faced with a situation that caused him to reexamine a previously accepted frame of reference and ultimately construct one that was much more inclusive. The discovery that his closest friends in seminary were gay was a disorienting experience that caused him to begin to "do research," as he said, and observe those within the gay community. While he did not say how long the process took, he began a critical assessment of his views, beliefs, and understandings as they related to homosexuality. He then explored new options, and over time his conviction grew as he was supported through additional experiences. Osmond also emphasized his depth of support for his sister and her female partner of twenty years. From his current perspective within society, he is an advocate for acceptance of same-sex relationships, though he remains mindful of his pastoral role. Thus efforts to remain balanced continue.

A collection of experiences over time helped to reshape his frame of reference. He is now better able to accommodate new information as it relates to homosexuality. In his case, the new frame enabled him to understand both supporters and detractors alike. His ability to frame, and then reframe the issue, was a key step in his learning process.

Osmond recognized the importance of reframing and stated quite plainly that one of his goals in helping congregants resolve issues is "to just help people widen their frame of reference." Osmond's experiences in seminary were emblematic of other clergy. A close personal relationship with gays altered the dynamics or helped to change the frame. While this was true for clergy, it also proved to be the case for congregants, family, and friends.

❀ CHAPTER 9 ❀

Focusing on the Fundamentals

Helping the Rest of Us Move Forward

It is understood that a full array of knowledge, skills, and attitudes are needed to successfully negotiate conflicts. Clergy responses and the strategies they mapped out for themselves can serve as guidelines and supports to other Episcopal clergy and others attempting to resolve similar conflicts. Faith was an essential component of the negotiation process. With this came an ability to become centered and emotionally aware in ways that allowed clergy to contextualize the problem and move forward to successfully resolve the conflict.

What's Faith Got to Do with It?

While it is very easy to become swept into the vortex of loud debates surrounding gay rights or many other hotly debated issues for that matter, it is often a nonproductive enterprise. It seems the greater the emotion involved, the less likely we are to actually hear what is being spoken. The path chosen by clergy as they resolved these conflicts was a cultivated path, a deliberately chosen path and one that required very conscious and sometimes counterintuitive steps.

We might expect experienced clergy to embark on such a journey, but how do the rest of us learn to take that first step? Many of the clergy interviewed had negotiated a number of conflicts and learned with each experience. What if I—artfully or inelegantly—often manage to dodge conflicts I should have tried to resolve? What if I am new to ministry and have no experience? Or what if I have years of experience negotiating conflicts in a totally different manner, a manner that runs counter to my faith? What if I am not a priest but grounded in another religious tradition? Can I use the experiences of clergy interviewed for this book if I eschew all religions but have a personal moral philosophy that informs my behavior? What can I take from this book that can be of use as I move forward when called to resolve conflicts?

There are key strategies that can be drawn from the experiences of clergy that may be useful in both secular and religious contexts. First, as Grant suggested, the idea is not to drown in the conflict. Those who were most successful were willing to get muddied and wet, but they also remained tethered to a force greater than the conflict itself. The arms out, palms open position is literal for priests as they stand at the altar, but it is also symbolic of remaining centered in whatever one places one's trust.

Being Centered

It is easy to attribute the perseverance of clergy to grace and faith. Yet in digging for a behavioral understanding, their ability to remain centered emerged as a key factor allowing for success. Negotiating emotional conflicts can be especially debilitating. Much can get in the way to take us off course. Seeking out whatever gives one peace and a relative amount of calm will help carry one through the inherent difficulties of resolving emotional conflicts. For Christians, this ability presumably comes as we are centered on a relationship with God. Even if one does not subscribe to this vision, however, there is still value in tapping into whatever power source provides one with grounding and peace—be it meditation, exercise, or some form of counsel. In order to negotiate especially difficult conflicts with greater ease, it is vital that one become psychologically and emotionally centered.

When one is centered, one is confident, not cocky, not overly confident, but balanced and responsive. Balance is not a fixed and motionless point. In order to maintain balance, one is actually constantly moving and making adjustments as needed, both large and small. Being able to reach one's center, however, makes achieving balance under a variety of conditions possible. By focusing on being centered, one is also able to cancel out the noise generated by assorted fears and to focus on priorities.

By assuming the posture of a priest, the individuals I spoke with became centered. Many skills and attitudes were incorporated into this posture, but an overall attitude of concern was by far the most prevalent. Clergy were compassionate, optimistic, trusting, made efforts to be inclusive, and held up the banner of social justice even in the face of anger and rejection. At times they displayed great vulnerability. Listening to their stories, I wondered how they had managed to maintain their compassion when, as Osmond described it, one sometimes wants to hold one's nose.

In terms of getting them through the difficult times, several priests spoke directly of their relationship with the Holy Spirit. An ability to assume a vulnerable position in the midst of conflict initially struck me as one of the more counterintuitive moves one could make. Yet the more I reflected on their approach, the more it seemed to be very much in alignment with a Christian worldview. For it was in their weakness and vulnerability that they drew strength from a greater power (2 Cor. 12:9–10).

Emotional Awareness

While it is not uncommon for emotions to factor into conflict negotiations, individuals may become especially emotional and uncomfortable when issues relating to sexuality are introduced. The highly emotional nature of conflicts over homosexuality cannot be ignored and must be framed appropriately in an attempt to respect all those involved in the conflict resolution. For some, conflicts over gay rights are a matter of social justice and not merely about sexuality. Nonetheless, this is not the perception of all parties, and emotional responses on all sides of a controversial issue must be acknowledged and addressed in order to reach resolutions.

The clergy I spoke with were mindful of the emotions of all those involved in negotiations, including the negotiator. Although the spiritual and emotional well-being of parishioners were a priority, clergy were cognizant of the personal toll such conflicts took on clergy themselves. They too needed to be fed. Being centered meant that they were fed by what they trusted most. By becoming centered, they were actually better able to manage their own emotional needs and maintain the most appropriate balance between the emotional dichotomy of personal and pastoral concerns.

Whether priest, deacon, layperson, or agnostic, invariably when facing conflicts we are torn between two opposing concerns in addition to the conflict itself. Coming to terms with our own inner struggles that precede our efforts to negotiate with others can help the immediate discussions as well as contribute to our long-term mental health.

Contextualizing the Problem

In their efforts to ensure that they did not drown in the conflict, clergy were successful when they contextualized the problem. It was often helpful to examine the conflict within the wider sphere of concerns. By understanding how they and others were affected by the environment and by appreciating the most important features of the landscape, they were able to take another constructive step forward. Identifying priorities is always helpful, but seeking out points of commonality is of special importance when one wants the relationships to remain intact over the long term. In such instances, the relationship itself becomes part of the larger context that can help parties temper hostilities.

While all parties have personalized goals, by not allowing oneself to become too narrowly focused on self interests, disputants may be able to encounter points of actual agreement in the larger sphere. It is these points of commonality that help bridge the differences needed to reach resolution. In stark contrast, the polarizing politics that took the United States to the brink of national default in the summer of 2011 stands as an extreme example of the antithesis of behavior designed to bring about a constructive resolution. Rather than locate their dispute within a larger nonpartisan context, Congress narrowly focused on individual political agendas, which only served to cement intransigence.

It has been said that the nature of politics today, with those on opposite sides spending less and less time together in social situations where genuine personal relationships are formed and deepened, has widened the divide and made it much more difficult to resolve conflicts. As we focus narrowly on our own positions, we are less likely to seek common ground and more likely to become intractable in the positions we hold. In the conflicts negotiated by clergy, the importance of social bonds emerged as a key issue leading to resolution.

Utilizing the Power of the Personal

By contextualizing the problem, clergy were better able to seek out the common ground that existed in spite of the dispute. Often that common ground centered on keeping relationships intact. Of all the lessons learned, I believe this was one of the most important. The power of the personal surfaced on two levels: the communal and the individual. Often the immediate conflict that related to gay rights included several individuals but had implications for the larger social group or parish. Thus it became a community issue.

Maintaining a dialogue and staying in relationship with the disaffected parties, as well as the *entire* network of individuals affected by the breach, helped clergy to reach a resolution that best served the community as a whole. The goal was for as many as possible to feel that their voices were heard. This increased the likelihood that they would support the ultimate solution. The genuine effort to engage individuals, regardless of their opinions, demonstrated in a tangible way that *all* were considered part of the community even if they concluded that they must agree to disagree. While clergy had an outcome in mind, that desired goal was superseded by the effort to care for the entire community.

This ability to ride the storms of a conflict by focusing on that which was more important than the points of disagreement was reflected in the actions of Connor, for example. He seemed to move through the conflicts he was called to negotiate with a tenacious love for those with whom he personally disagreed. By making his parish gay-friendly, he initially alienated some of his parishioners. In the process he took many risks, but he did not lose sight of his primary focus. He spent a great deal of time communicating with those within the parish. There were many dinners where they talked, listened, disagreed, and tried to explain where they were headed and why. Interestingly enough, despite his unwavering support for gays, his chief concern was not for the inclusion of gays within the church, but for his relationship with parishioners. That concern was a focus and outweighed many aspects of the disputes. Connor said:

> My biggest challenge was to help people know that I loved them. What the older people came to understand was that "when I get sick, Connor will be there. I may disagree with everything he's saying right now, but over three or four or five years he's going to be my pastor and he's not going to let me down." So when there were family crises, I just became a pastor. And out of all that they could stand up and say, "I totally disagree with you, but I know you love me and I love you and we're going to work this out." So it became that kind of a journey with some people.

The conflict resolution experiences of clergy were analogous to a journey that encompassed many paths. Sometimes the path was lengthy. Sometimes the changes were profound, but those who were most successful in resolving disputes did not allow the dispute to over-shadow higher-level concerns for one another as Christians. Change and growth emerged as clergy chose a path that allowed them to focus on the relationships as priorities as they moved forward to reach their ultimate goal.

Inclusive efforts sent out a very positive message to the communities engaged in the conflict negotiations. As Ellen said, when in the midst of negotiating a conflict, one cannot be effective by simply sitting in the office and making up rules. In Connie's experience, efforts to embrace the entire group of individuals affected by the conflict made them feel better about the outcome even if the outcome was not what they would have ideally chosen.

The power of the personal also emerged on an individual level. Clergy who developed individual personal relationships with gays seemed better able to succeed in their efforts to negotiate conflicts relating to gay rights. It is not clear if this stemmed from an incentive as advocate, or because it enabled clergy to look beyond the differences and embrace the human rights. In any event, meaningful personal contact and the development of personal relationships between gay and straight men and women significantly altered the dynamics surrounding the conflict.

As perceptions were changed, conversations gradually moved away from "hot-button" rhetoric. Once individuals move beyond speech making and enter into a genuinely personal discourse, actions may then be altered. The absence of such personal connections increases the tendency to compartmentalize the issues and distance oneself from the human element involved. On the other hand, the ability to identify with the other point of view contributes to the resolution of the conflict. It may help individuals reframe the issues involved and increase their empathy for individuals on both sides of the conflict. Straight clergy indicated that their personal evolution concerning the rights of gays allowed them to identify with gays as well as those who struggle with accepting gay rights.

Getting There

Never have I met a person named Shadrach, nor Meshach, nor Abednego. I imagine it is because few mothers want to envision their children walking through flames, regardless of the outcome. Yet, with regard to developing the skills needed to resolve conflicts, one must be willing to step into the fiery furnace of negotiations in order to become effective. If only we could remember that we need not walk through that furnace alone. Repeatedly clergy demonstrated how they gained strength by assuming an arms out, palms open posture.

In addition, clergy relayed incidents that showed how lessons learned informally through experience were among the most memorable. These experiences had the greatest impact on their lives and enabled them to improve their negotiation skills. Regardless of whether or not clergy had received formal training, informal learning through interactions with others was a preferred and effective approach to learning how to negotiate conflicts. Those who had benefited from formal training were able to refine their skills through informal means. These seat-of-your-pants informal strategies that helped clergy develop a reservoir of skills are available to a wider audience if only we are willing to take that first step.

Perhaps the bravest step taken by clergy, and at the same time the most freeing, was the choice to abandon fear. When we are afraid, we often fail to listen to the many decibels of sound being uttered. When fearful, we are often more concerned with convincing those across the table that we are right and they are wrong. As negotiators operating from a place of fear, we freeze or fumble as we anticipate our short-comings. Yet as Osmond suggested, love truly can alleviate our fears:

> The arms out . . . palms open is not only the *orans* [Latin— praying] posture . . . but it is also the beginning of intimacy . . . of embrace . . . of inclusion. It is cruciform. . . . It models for us the One we call Love. But people who are afraid will cringe, cower, shrink, duck, and fold up. It is love that conquers fear and enables us to open our arms, our palms—and our hearts.

It is only as we are willing to become vulnerable that we can attempt to love our way through to a better outcome. Love then becomes the guiding force that propels us toward the ultimate resolution.

Bibliography

Andrade, L., D. A. Plowman, and D. Duchon. "Getting Past Conflict Resolution: A Complexity View of Conflict." *Emergence Complexity & Organization* 10, no. 1 (2008): 23–38.

Anglican Communion Official Website. http://www.anglicancommunion.org/.

Armentrout, D. S., and R. B. Slocum. *An Episcopal Dictionary of the Church: A User-Friendly Reference for Episcopalians.* New York: Church Publishing, 2000.

Arnau, L. "Whether Building a Kitchen or Building a Learning Team, Collaboration Is Key." *Journal of Staff Development* 30, no. 1 (2009): 59–60.

Bacal, R. "Organizational Conflict: The Good, the Bad and the Ugly." *Journal for Quality and Participation* 27, no. 2 (2004): 21–22.

Baker, J. "A Whole New School: The Art of Reflection, Innovation, Transformation." *Independent School* 68, no. 3 (2009): 30–32, 34–36, 38.

Bandura, A. *Social Learning Theory.* Upper Saddle River, NJ: Prentice Hall, 1977.

Banerjee, N. "Episcopal Diocese Votes to Secede." *The New York Times,* December 9, 2007. http://www.nytimes.com

Beebe, R. "Predicting Burnout, Conflict Management Style, and Turnover among Clergy." *Journal of Career Assessment* 15, no. 2 (2007): 257–75.

Benner, P., and M. Sutphen. "Learning across the Professions: The Clergy, a Case in Point." *Journal of Nursing Education* 46, no. 3 (2007): 103–8.

Black, V. *Welcome to the Church Year: An Introduction to the Seasons of the Episcopal Church.* Harrisburg, PA: Morehouse Publishing, 2004.

Bloomberg, L., and M. Volpe. *Completing Your Qualitative Dissertation: A Roadmap from Beginning to End.* Los Angeles: Sage Publications, 2008.

Boone, E. J., R. D. Safrit, and J. Jones. *Developing Programs in Adult Education: A Conceptual Programming Model.* Prospect Heights, IL: Waveland Press, 2002.

Boorstein, M. "Longtime Bishop Who Presided over Va. Rift to Step Down." *The Washington Post,* January 24, 2009. http://www.washingtonpost.com.

Booth, W., G. Colomb, and J. Williams. *The Craft of Research.* Chicago: University of Chicago Press, 2003.

Boud, D. "Experiential Living." In *International Encyclopedia of Adult Education,* edited by L. English, 243–45. New York: Palgrave, 2005.

Bourner, T. "Assessing Reflective Learning." *Education and Training* 45, no. 5 (2003): 267–72.

Boyd, E., and A. Fales. "Reflective Learning." *Journal of Humanistic Psychology* 23, no. 2 (1983): 99–117.

Burns, R., and R. Cervero. "How Pastors Learn the Politics of Ministry Practice." *Religious Education* 97, no. 4 (2002): 304–21.

Cadge, W., L. Olson, and C. Wildeman. "How Denominational Resources Influence Debates about Homosexuality in Mainline Protestant Congregations." *Sociology of Religion* 69, no. 2 (2008): 187–207.

Cadge, W., and C. Wildeman. "Facilitators and Advocates: How Mainline Protestant Clergy Respond to Homosexuality." *Sociological Perspectives* 51, no. 3 (2008): 587–603.

Callanan, G. A., and D. Perri. "Teaching Conflict Management Using a Scenario-Based Approach." *Journal of Education for Business* 81, no. 3 (2006): 131–39.

Cannell, P. "Vygotsky's Educational Theory in Cultural Context." *British Journal of Educational Technology* 35, no. 3 (2004): 385.

Cole, M., V. John-Steiner, S. Scribner, and E. Souberman, eds. *Mind in Society: Development of Higher Psychological Processes.* Cambridge, MA: Harvard University Press, 1978.

Cranton, P. *Understanding and Promoting Transformative Learning.* San Francisco: Jossey-Bass, 2006.

Creswell, J. W. *Qualitative Inquiry and Research Design: Choosing among Five Traditions.* Thousand Oaks, CA: Sage Publications, 1998.

Crew, L. *101 Reasons to Be Episcopalian.* Harrisburg, PA: Morehouse Publishing, 2003.

Da Costa, J. L. (2006). "Changing an Adult Learning Environment as Viewed from a Social Learning Perspective." *International Electronic Journal for Leadership in Learning* 10, no. 1 (2006): 1.

Dana, D. *Conflict Resolution.* New York: McGraw-Hill, 2001.

Danforth, J. *Faith and Politics: How the Moral Values Debate Divides America and How to Move Forward Together.* New York: Viking, 2006.

Daudelin, M.W. "Learning from Experience through Reflection." In *Strategic Learning in a Knowledge Economy,* edited by R. Cross and S. Israelit, 297–312. Boston: Butterworth-Heinemann, 2000.

Deutsch, M., P. Coleman, and E. Marcus, eds. *The Handbook of Conflict Resolution.* San Francisco: Jossey-Bass, 2006.

Deutsch, M., and J. Goldman. "A Framework for Thinking about Research on Conflict Resolution Initiatives." In *The Handbook of Conflict Resolution,* edited by M. Deutsch, P. T. Coleman, and E. C. Marcus, 825–48. San Francisco: Jossey-Bass, 2006.

Dewey, J. *Experience and Education.* New York: Touchstone, 1997.

Dyke, M. "An Enabling Framework for Reflexive Learning: Experiential Learning and Reflexivity in Contemporary Modernity." *International Journal of Lifelong Education* 28, no. 3 (2009): 289–310.

Episcopal Church Official Website. http://www.episcopalchurch.org.

Episcopal Congregations Overview Charts 2008. http://www.episcopalchurch.org/documents/Episcopal_Congregations_Overview_Charts.ppt.

The Episcopal Diocese of New Hampshire Official Website. http://www.nhepiscopal.org/bishop/bishop.html.

Episcopal Overview: Fact 2008. http://www.episcopalchurch.org/documents/Episcopal_Overview_FACT_2008.pdf.

Fisher, R., and W. Ury. *Getting to Yes: Negotiating Agreement without Giving In.* 2nd ed. New York: Houghton Mifflin Company, 1991.

Fischer-Yoshida, B., and I. Wasserman. "Moral Conflict and Engaging Alternative Perspectives." In *The Handbook of Conflict Resolution*, edited by M. Deutsch, P. T. Coleman, and E. C. Marcus, 560–81. San Francisco: Jossey-Bass, 2006.

Foster, C., L. Dahill, L. Golemon, and B. Wang Tolentino. *Educating Clergy: Teaching Practices and Pastoral Imagination.* San Francisco: Jossey-Bass, 2005.

Fowler, J. *Stages of Faith.* San Francisco: Harper Collins, 1981.

Galli, M. "Is the Gay Marriage Debate Over?" *Christianity Today* 53, no. 7 (2009): 30–33.

Glassgold, J., and S. Knapp. "Ethical Issues in Screening Clergy or Candidates for Religious Professions for Denominations That Exclude Homosexual Clergy." *Professional Psychology: Research and Practice* 39, no. 3 (2008): 346–52.

Goodstein, L. "Episcopal Bishops Give Ground on Gay Marriage." *New York Times,* July 16, 2009. http://www.nytimes.com/2009/07/16/us/16episcopal.html.

———. "Episcopalians Confirm a Second Gay Bishop." *New York Times,* March 17, 2010. http://www.nytimes.com/2010/03/18/us/18bishop.html.

———. "First Openly Gay Episcopal Bishop to Retire." *New York Times,* November 6, 2010. http://www.nytimes.com/2010/11/07/us/07bishop.html.

Grein, R. *Continuing the Dialogue: A Pastoral Study Document of the House of Bishops to the Church as the Church Considers Issues of Human Sexuality.* Cincinnati: Forward Movement Publications, 1995.

Grossman, R. "Structures for Facilitating Student Reflection." *College Teaching* 57, no. 1 (2008): 15–22.

Groves, P., ed. *The Anglican Communion and Homosexuality: The Official Study Guide to Enable Listening and Dialogue.* London: SPCK Publishing, 2007.

Grusec, J. E. "Social Learning Theory and Developmental Psychology: The Legacies of Robert Sears and Albert Bandura." *Developmental Psychology* 28 (1992): 776–86.

Harvey, T., and B. Drolet. *Building Teams, Building People: Expanding the Fifth Resource.* Lanham, MD: Rowman & Littlefield Education, 2006.

Hassett, M. *Anglican Communion in Crisis: How Episcopal Dissidents and Their African Allies Are Reshaping Anglicanism.* New Jersey: Princeton University Press, 2007.

Hawkins, J. B., and I. Markham. "The Episcopal Church and the Anglican Communion." *Modern Believing* 49, no. 3 (2008): 17–25.

Hawtrey, K. "Using Experiential Learning Techniques." *Journal of Economic Education* 38, no. 2 (2007): 143–52.

Hillerbrand, H. J., ed. *The Encyclopedia of Protestantism*. 1st ed. Routledge Reference Resources online. http://www.reference.routledge.com/subscriber/entry?entry=w028_e370.

Holmes, D. *A Brief History of the Episcopal Church*. Harrisburg, PA: Trinity Press International, 1993.

Howell, C. "Democratic Education and Social Learning Theory". *Philosophy of Education Yearbook*. (2005): 161–70.

Jamieson, P. "The Serious Matter of Informal Learning." *Planning for Higher Education* 37, no. 2 (2009): 18–25.

Jarvis, P. *Democracy, Lifelong Learning, and the Learning Society: Active Citizenship in a Late Modern Age*. London: Routledge, 2008.

———. "Religious Experience and Experiential Learning." *Religious Education* 103, no. 5 (2008): 553–67.

Johnson, D., and R. Johnson. "Energizing Learning: The Instructional Power of Conflict." *Educational Researcher* 38, no. 1 (2009): 37–51.

Kerlinger, F., and H. Lee. *Foundations of Behavioral Research*. South Melbourne, Australia: Thomson Learning, 2000.

Keysar, A. *American Religious Identification Survey*. New York: Graduate Center of the City of New York, 2001. http://www.gc.cuny.edu/faculty/research_briefs/aris/key_findings.htm.

Kilduff, K. "The Interpersonal Structure of Decision Making: A Social Comparison Approach to Organizational Choice." *Organizational Behavior and Human Decision Processes* 47, no. 2 (1990): 270–88.

Kolb, D. A. *Experimental Learning: Experience as the Source of Learning and Development*. Englewood Cliffs, NJ: Prentice Hall, 1984.

Kosmin, B. A., and E. Mayer. *American Religious Identification Survey*. New York: Graduate Center of the City of New York, 2001.

Kramer, J. "A Canterbury Tale." *The New Yorker*, April 26, 2011. http://www.newyorker.com/reporting/2010/04/26/100426fa_fact_kramer.

Krauss, R., and E. Morsella. "Communication and Conflict." In *The Handbook of Conflict Resolution,* edited by M. Deutsch, P. T. Coleman, and E. C. Marcus, 144–57. San Francisco: Jossey-Bass, 2006.

Kriesberg, L. *Constructive Conflicts*. 3rd ed. Lanham, MD: Rowman & Littlefield, 2007.

Lee, M. "Collaborative Learning." In *International Encyclopedia of Adult Education,* edited by L. English, 117–22. New York: Pallgrave Macmillan, 2005.

Lewicki, R. J. "Trust, Trust Development, and Trust Repair." In *The Handbook of Conflict Resolution*, edited by M. Deutsch, P. T. Coleman, and E. C. Marcus, 92–119. San Francisco: Jossey-Bass, 2006.

Lewicki, R. J., D. M. Saunders, B. Barry, and J. Minton. *Essentials of Negotiation*. 3rd ed. New York: Irwin McGraw-Hill, 2004.

Lindner, E. "Emotion and Conflict." In *The Handbook of Conflict Resolution*, edited by M. Deutsch, P. T. Coleman, and E. C. Marcus, 268–93. San Francisco: Jossey-Bass, 2006.

Malony, H. N. "Ministerial Effectiveness: A Review of Recent Research." *Pastoral Psychology* 33, no. 2 (1984): 96–104.

———. "The Psychological Evaluation of Religious Professionals." *Professional Psychology: Research and Practice* 31, no. 5 (2000): 521–25.

Marshall, C., and G. Rossman. *Designing Qualitative Research.* Thousand Oaks, CA: Sage Publications, 1999.

Marsick, V. "Learning in the Workplace: The Case for Reflectivity and Critical Reflectivity." *Adult Education Quarterly* 38, no. 4 (1988): 187–98.

Marsick, V. J., A. Sauquet, and L. Yorks. "Learning through Reflection." In *The Handbook of Conflict Resolution,* edited by M. Deutsch, P. T. Coleman, and E. C. Marcus, 486–506. San Francisco: Jossey-Bass, 2006.

Marsick, V., and K. Watkins. *Facilitating Learning Organizations.* Brookfield, VT: Gower, 1999.

———. *Informal and Incidental Learning in the Workplace.* New York: Routledge, 1990.

Merriam, S. *Qualitative Research and Case Study Applications in Education.* San Francisco: Jossey-Bass, 1998.

Mezirow, J. "Learning to Think Like an Adult: Core Concepts of Transformation Theory." In *Transformative Dimensions of Adult Learning,* 3–33. San Francisco: Jossey-Bass, 2000.

———. *Transformative Dimensions of Adult Learning.* San Francisco: Jossey-Bass, 1991.

Moix, B. "Matters of Faith: Religion, Conflict, and Conflict Resolution." In *The Handbook of Conflict Resolution,* edited by M. Deutsch, P. T. Coleman, and E. C. Marcus, 582–601. San Francisco: Jossey-Bass, 2006.

Morgan, T. C. "Defending the Faith." *Christianity Today* 52, no. 10 (2008): 92.

———. "Global Ultimatum: The Larger Meaning of Anglican Leader's Demand That the Episcopal Church Change Its Ways." *Christianity Today* 51, no. 4 (2007): 74–77.

Murphy, M. "Compassionate Communication Circles at FOR." *Witness: A Newsletter of the Fellowship of Reconciliation* (2009): 2.

Ontario Consultants on Religious Tolerance Glossary of Religious and Spiritual Terms. http://www.religioustolerance.org/gl_f.htm.

Preciphs, T. K. "Understanding Adult Learning for Social Action in a Volunteer Setting." PhD diss., 1989. Retrieved from ProQuest 74455261/AAT.

Priestley, T. L. "Learning to Unlearn: A Case Study of the Initial Rejection and Subsequent Acceptance of Homosexuality by Heterosexuals." PhD diss., Columbia University, 2009. Retrieved from ProQuest 1850867301/AAT 3368425.

Pruitt, D. G. "Social Conflict." In *Handbook of Social Psychology,* edited by D. Gilbert, S. T. Fiske, and G. Lindzey, 470–503. 4th ed. New York: McGraw Hill, 1998.

Rahim, M. *Managing Conflict in Organizations.* Westport, CT: Quorum Books, 2001.

Robson, C. *Real World Research: A Resource for Social Scientists and Practitioner Researchers.* Malden, MA: Blackwell Publishing, 2002.

Schellenberg, J. *Conflict Resolution: Theory, Research, and Practice.* Albany: State University of New York Press, 1996.

Schon, D. *The Reflective Practitioner: How Professionals Think in Action.* London: Temple Smith, 1983.

Sorensen, A. "Social Learning and Health Plan Choice." *Rand Journal of Economics* 37, no. 4 (2006): 929–45.

Trounson, R. "Church Divide over Gays Has a Global Audience: As the Anglican Debate Plays Out, Other Denominations Seek Guidance for Similar Battles in Their Future." *Los Angeles Times,* October 14, 2007, A-16.

Turner, P. "An Unworkable Theology." *First Things* 154 (June/July 2005): 10–12.

Waks, L. "Listening and Reflecting: An Introduction to the Special Issue." *Learning Inquiry* 1, no. 2 (2007): 83–87.

Waldman, S. *Founding Faith: Providence, Politics, and the Birth of Religious Freedom in America.* New York: Random House, 2008.

Webber, C. *Welcome to the Episcopal Church: An Introduction to Its History, Faith, and Worship.* Harrisburg, PA: Morehouse Publishing, 1999.

Westerhoff, J. *Living Faithfully as a Prayer Book People.* Harrisburg, PA: Morehouse Publishing, 2004.

———. *Will Our Children Have Faith?* Harrisburg, PA: Morehouse Publishing, 2000.

Wildemeersch, D., and J. Vandenabeele. "Relocating Social Learning as a Democratic Practice." In *Democratic Practices as Learning Opportunities*, edited by R. van der Veen, D. Wildemeersch, J. Youngblood, and V. Marsick, 19–32. Rotterdam, Netherlands: Sense Publishers, 2007.

Yin, R. "Case Study Research." *Applied Social Research Methods Series* 5. Thousand Oaks, CA: Sage Publications, 2003.

Zagenczyk, T., R. Gibney, A. Murrell, and S. Boss. "Friends Don't Make Friends Good Citizens, but Advisors Do." *Group & Organization Management* 33 (2008): 760–80.

Index